HOW TO BE
THE BEST
VOLUNTEER YOUTH WORKER
IN THE HISTORY OF THE WORLD

KURT JOHNSTON

HOW TO BE **THE BEST**
VOLUNTEER YOUTH WORKER
IN THE HISTORY OF THE WORLD

Copyright © 2020 Kurt Johnston
Publisher: Mark Oestreicher
Managing Editor: Sarah Hauge
Cover Design: Adam McLane
Layout: Marilee Pankratz
Creative Director: Valerie Unteer

All rights reserved. No part of this book may be reproduced in any form by any electronic or mechanical means including photocopying, recording, or information storage and retrieval without permission in writing from the author.

Unless otherwise indicated, all Scripture quotations are taken from the Holy Bible, New Living Translation, copyright © 1996, 2004, 2015 by Tyndale House Foundation. Used by permission of Tyndale House Publishers, Inc., Carol Stream, Illinois 60188. All rights reserved.

Scripture quotations marked (NIV) are taken from the Holy Bible, New International Version®, NIV®. Copyright © 1973, 1978, 1984, 2011 by Biblica, Inc.® Used by permission. All rights reserved worldwide.

ISBN-13: 978-1-942145-53-0

The Youth Cartel, LLC
www.theyouthcartel.com
Email: info@theyouthcartel.com
Born in San Diego.
Printed in the U.S.A.

CONTENTS

INTRODUCTION	5
CHAPTER 1: **Keep Jesus at the Center**	7
CHAPTER 2: **Embrace the Squiggle**	15
CHAPTER 3: **Improve Your Serve**	25
CHAPTER 4: **Be a Team Player**	35
CHAPTER 5: **Help Parents Win**	45
CHAPTER 6: **Be Interested, Not Interesting**	53
CHAPTER 7: **Master the Three Key Skills**	59
CHAPTER 8: **Teach Like It Actually Matters**	67
CHAPTER 9: **Don't Get Deflated By Flat Tires**	77
CHAPTER 10: **Stick Around**	87
ENDNOTES	95

Dedicated to Paul Dempster

You've traveled to Hong Kong to help train youth workers.

You've patiently put up with me as a junior high small group coleader.

You've opened your home countless times.

You've paid for students to go to camp.

You've 'Zoomed' with students for more than FIFTY nights in a row during the global pandemic of 2020.

Paul, you have gone above and beyond for years and our youth ministry is better because of you!

You are, without a doubt, the second-greatest volunteer youth worker in the history of the world. Who's number one? You should know...you're married to her!

An Introduction

Not long ago I was speaking to a group of teenagers when I said, "You know, I'm of the opinion that being really good at stuff is overrated!" At the time, we were in the middle of an event dedicated to helping teens get excited about using their gifts to make a difference in the world. That message is at the heart of much of youth ministry. The world is rife with opportunities for young people to step up, step out, and step into various chances to contribute. But teenagers are often hesitant to do so because they are afraid they won't get it right; they fear they'll fumble the ball or drop it completely. They've bought into the lie that unless you can be really good at something, it's not worth the effort. I have a different opinion. I think being really good is, very often, overrated. The effort is what counts! And that's what I wanted to convey to teenagers with my simple statement.

Of course, there are exceptions. I'm glad my surgeon is really good at surgeon stuff. When my wife and I decided to hire a professional to paint the interior of our house, we wouldn't have been satisfied with somebody who sucked at painting but put in a good effort. Sometimes being really good at stuff is actually really good!

Enter youth ministry. Enter you. You might be a veteran youth worker, or reading this book might be your first foray into the world of ministry to teenagers. Either way, I'm glad you are taking the time to read about youth ministry and how you can be really good at it…maybe even the best volunteer youth worker in the history of the world! That bold claim is impossible to substantiate. But like I said earlier, there are times when being really good at stuff is actually really good. I think that's true of youth ministry. Getting better at youth ministry is worth the effort because teenagers are worth the effort. I think you believe that, too, which is why you picked up this little book in the first place.

Thanks for volunteering in what I believe is the most important ministry in the church! Thanks for stepping into a ministry that most adults run from! Thanks for believing teenagers are worth the effort!

I hope this little book helps you become really good at youth ministry….maybe even the best volunteer youth worker in the history of the world! Hey, somebody has to claim that title, why not you?

How This Book Works. It's Quite Simple:

- There are ten topics, broken into ten chapters
- Each chapter starts with a quick intro
- That's followed by the "Three Biggies in a Box"
- Those are followed by an explanation of each "Biggie"
- Each chapter has a sidebar written by an amazing volunteer youth worker
- Read this book in order, or jump around
- When you are finished, you will be well on your way to becoming the best volunteer youth worker in the history of the world

CHAPTER 1
KEEP JESUS AT THE CENTER

A few years ago I had a sobering experience. I was conducting about a dozen interviews with teenagers who had grown up in our youth ministry and now wanted to be summer interns. For the most part, these college-aged young adults had once been considered core members of our youth group, claimed to have a strong faith, and felt called to ministry. They were the cream of the crop. At some point in every interview, I would ask the candidate to talk to me about Jesus. When did they become a Christ-follower? How would they tell others about him? Why is a relationship with Christ so important? What sets Jesus apart from other religious figures in history? This was where the wheels began to fall off the cart. Across the board, with only a few exceptions, the cream of our youth ministry crop—college students called to ministry—couldn't formulate articulate responses to what seemed like fairly simple inquiries. I was shocked. They loved God, loved the local church, loved youth ministry, and loved Jesus. Yet they knew very little about him and could barely verbalize what they did know. Yikes!

What does my eye-opening moment have to do with your youth ministry role at your church? A ton.

One of the most important responsibilities of the youth worker is to be a role model; a mentor. At its core, youth work is about building relationships with teenagers and helping them grow and maintain a relationship with Jesus. And because of that, it's vital that youth ministries be chock-full of adults who each have a vibrant, fresh, mature, and growing walk with Christ themselves. The formal programs your youth group offers are important pieces of the puzzle, but too often too much trust is placed in those programs. When functioning at their best, programs (Sunday school, mid-week gatherings, small groups, student leadership teams, camps, events, etc.) mostly serve as vehicles to get adults and teenagers interacting. The programs set the table for relational youth ministry. Our youth ministry had put too much faith in our programs and assumed the awesome programs were doing an awesome job of developing well-rounded, confident followers of Jesus. The interviews with our potential interns who had grown up under our roof proved otherwise. Programs are pointless unless they help connect teenagers with "Jesus-freaky" adults!

3 BIGGIES IN A BOX

IT'S ALL ABOUT JESUS
YOU + JESUS + TEENAGER = GOOD MINISTRY
LIVE AND LEAD LIKE JESUS

It's All About Jesus

Ultimately, every church youth group is in the business of introducing teenagers to Jesus. How that looks from group to group varies based on a host of factors such as theology, methodology, personal bent of the leader of the youth ministry, etc. But if your ministry doesn't have pointing students to Jesus as its ultimate goal, it may as well be a YMCA. Don't get me wrong, I love the YMCA. But it isn't supposed to be a church, or vice versa.

So what did we do when we realized our youth ministry wasn't pointing teenagers to Jesus the way we assumed it was? Well, we're still working on it, but we started by deciding to infuse Jesus into every possible aspect of our ministry. We immediately made three changes that helped ensure that Jesus was always the "True North" of our ministry:

1. We added Jesus to our purpose statement and changed our in-house youth ministry training and strategy to begin with, "Our ministry has Jesus as its center." Until then it had been assumed that everybody knew Jesus was our focus, but the reality is that while he was in the picture, he wasn't front and center.

2. We determined to move from a mentality of "….and, Jesus" (doing a bunch of good stuff AND adding Jesus into the mix) to one of "Jesus, and…." (starting with Jesus as the center and adding other stuff into the mix). Semantics? Perhaps. But sometimes how we say things makes all the difference.

3. We coined an intentionally controversial new phrase: "Less God; More Jesus." If that phrase has you scratching your head or makes you wonder what seminary I attended… it's done its job! Let me briefly explain. While interviewing our potential interns, I quickly realized that they all loved God and believed God was the answer to most of what ails humankind. In the interviews, there was much "God talk" and almost no mention of Jesus until I brought him into the conversation, and then they couldn't articulate much about him. My takeaway: Many church kids know a lot about God but not nearly enough about Jesus. Most unchurched teenagers aren't atheists, but have a belief in, and even an appreciation of, "God." The generic "god" that shows up from religion to religion is, for the most part, a welcomed and appreciated concept. Despite various efforts, removing "In God We Trust" from U.S. currency has failed time and time again. Why? Generally speaking, Americans like God. But collectively we know very little about Jesus. So our youth ministry decided that whenever we could, and whenever it made sense, we would substitute "God talk" for "Jesus talk," or at the very least insert Jesus language into virtually every aspect of our ministry, from the messages to the casual conversations.

HOW TO BE **THE BEST** VOLUNTEER YOUTH WORKER

I have to admit that writing this first little section has been embarrassing. I have the privilege of leading what is widely considered one of the most successful and influential youth ministries in the world, but under my watch we were failing to do the most important thing a youth group is supposed to do. We failed to make sure it was ALL about Jesus.

You + Jesus + Teenager = Good Youth Ministry

It's been said that leaders are learners, and I tend to agree. As a volunteer youth leader, you need to have the mindset of being a lifelong learner, continuously sharpening the saw. And toward that end there are a myriad of conferences, workshops, blogs, podcasts, and books that can help you hone your youth ministry understanding and skills. Keep learning! But don't overthink it. Youth ministry isn't rocket science and you don't need a seminary degree to be an incredible youth worker.

In our setting we constantly remind our team of the recipe, or equation, for good youth ministry: Caring Adult + Jesus + Teenager = Good Youth Ministry. It can't be that simple, can it? Yes! Put most simply, youth ministry is about adults who love Jesus allowing their lives to intersect with teenagers' lives, with the hope of pointing those teenagers toward a life-changing relationship with Jesus.

When I was in junior high, I attended a tiny youth group that consisted of exactly three of us: me, my best friend Mike Pace, and a girl (sorry, girl, I can't remember your name). Our youth "room" was large enough to fit a three-cushion couch for the three of us and a chair for our leader, John Miller, to sit in. John was in his mid-twenties and newly married, and he grinded out long, physical days in a blue-collar job. He had no formal ministry training, he was rarely prepared to teach the lesson, and he had no clue how to answer about 99% of our questions. But John LOVED Jesus. He was constantly talking about Jesus and the impact he'd made on John's young marriage, and his outlook at work and life in general. The guy wouldn't shut up about Jesus! Additionally,

KEEP JESUS AT THE CENTER

John seemed to genuinely care about me, Mike, and the girl (sorry again, girl). He and his wife would invite us over to their apartment for swim parties, he'd show up at my football games, and he even bought an extra dirt bike so he could take me and Mike motorcycle riding.

John moved when we were in eighth grade and I quit attending church. The next three years or so proved to be the toughest, rowdiest, most regrettable years of my life. It wasn't until my junior year in high school that somebody reached out and invited me to another youth group in town. The only reason I was open to going was that I remembered a guy named John Miller who really loved Jesus and truly cared about me, Mike, and the girl (once again, sorry, girl). A few months after returning to church I gave my life to Christ. The reality is that John Miller did most of the heavy lifting. The love he had for Jesus and the way he allowed his life to intersect with mine were preparing my heart to be open to the gospel years later. My story is a living example of Jesus's parable of the four soils. John was working hard, plowing away at hard soil, softening it into soil that would someday be receptive to the seed another youth worker would sow.

Today, the youth ministry I help lead meets in a 50,000 square foot facility and has all the bells and whistles a youth group could ever hope for. We've got basketball courts, a skate park, a sand volleyball court, pool tables, lights, cameras, and action…gosh, we've got a lot of action.

And NONE of it is required to make good youth ministry happen!

The only things required to make good youth ministry happen are YOU + JESUS + TEENAGER.

It was good enough for John Miller way back in 1980, and it's good enough for you today.

Live And Lead Like Jesus

Teenagers are coming of age in a world that, generally speaking, is less open-minded about faith than the one you and I grew up in. Christianity is misrepresented and misunderstood (we've largely got ourselves to blame for that, but I digress). Men and women of faith are increasingly expected to sit down, shut up, and keep their beliefs to themselves. Because of this, the teenagers in your youth group need to see adults living a "loud and proud" life of faith. I'm not suggesting you go grab a bullhorn and head to the streets, or that being loud and proud means being obnoxious, arrogant, and smug. I'm simply suggesting that the teens in your youth group desperately need to see adult men and women who are proud of their faith, who allow their walk with Jesus to influence their lives in tangible ways. If you live as a closeted Christian, why would the teenagers you lead live any differently?

You probably remember the old WWJD bracelets. The bracelets have long gone out of style, but I think there are still some fair questions for adult followers of Jesus to ask themselves regularly, in addition to "What would Jesus do?":

- What would Jesus say?
- What would Jesus value?
- Who would Jesus seek out?
- Who would Jesus speak up for?
- How would Jesus respond?

As a volunteer youth worker, you are a role model. The apostle Paul's admonishment to "follow me as I follow Christ" is one we should aspire to as well. Our walk of faith—our journey with Jesus—should serve as an example to the teenagers in our youth ministries.

Side note: Being an example doesn't mean you're perfect. Life is messy and following Jesus doesn't automatically make it cleaner. One of the most effective ways to live and lead like Jesus is to do so in the midst of the mess and the muck. How you bounce back

KEEP JESUS AT THE CENTER

after a setback, how you navigate pain, loss, and disappointment, and how you stay faithful to Christ in the darkest of seasons are all vital to model to your teens.

THOUGHTS FROM A VOLUNTEER
by Teresa Genoway

Having become a Christian in my teenage years, I quickly mastered what I thought life with Christ should look like: obeying the rules and doing good to others. This was easy for me, as I am a rule-follower at heart. Little did I realize my black-and-white thinking served as a poor witness of Christ to others because it communicated a lot of judgment with little love. Later, a crisis in my personal life put me on a path to recovery from legalistic Christianity—a journey of loving Jesus with all of my being. My whole life changed as I learned to be a Jesus-follower, not a rule-follower. This has impacted how I shepherd the teenagers under my care. I don't want them to just know the Bible, I want them to know Jesus.

No matter what topic we discuss, my goal is to always point teenagers back to Jesus. I encourage them to know that life with Jesus works from the inside out. Falling in love with him comes first, and it results in our outward lives being transformed to his image. I share my own struggles, detailing how my relationship with Jesus has not only brought comfort but has increased my faith. As teens navigate difficult cultural issues, I turn their attention to the Gospels, letting Jesus himself inform their worldview. I let them know that if we get the rules right but get Jesus wrong, we get true life wrong. I admit, at times I can come across as a little goofy and over-the-top when I talk about Jesus, but my greatest desire is for teenagers to know Jesus and make him known. In a culture that screams "You do you," I encourage them to "Do Jesus" instead, following his example of loving others like he loved them.

I have had to learn to be patient with young people through their process of loving Jesus, realizing that it took much too long for Jesus to get my own attention. Just as seeds planted in one season yield fruit in a different one, I have had to be faithful in leading even when the ground looks barren, realizing that God is doing an "inside" job. It is also important for me to cultivate my own relationship with Jesus as I lead others to do the same. As Jesus infiltrates my being, I become winsome and am able to have influence over those under my care. This gift of pointing others toward a growing, thriving, and loving relationship with Jesus is like no other; I am always humbled that God has given me the privilege of shepherding this next generation of Jesus-followers. In so doing, the commission given by Jesus in Matthew 28:19 is realized and disciples are made, bringing glory to God.

Teresa Genoway has been a high school volunteer youth worker for nine years. When not talking about Jesus, she enjoys cooking and gardening and is always happy to share a meal and a bouquet of flowers with her high schoolers! She has been married to Jeff for thirty-three years and is a mother to four grown children.

CHAPTER 2
EMBRACE THE SQUIGGLE

Youth ministry is tough. And while all sorts of things contribute to make it tough, the biggest factor is teenagers! I mean, seriously, youth ministry would be so much easier if it wasn't for teenagers.

But, alas, teenagers ARE a fairly important part of youth ministry. And here's one of the best lessons I've learned over the course of my career: Understanding adolescent development and embracing the journey all teenagers find themselves on is the key to feeling less frustrated as a youth worker. Conversely, a failure to understand these things will lead to repeated feelings of frustration and ineffectiveness.

I like pictures, and this feels like a good place to explain myself using a very sophisticated visual aid.

Many adults think a teenager's spiritual journey should look like this.

We've bought into the idea that if we are good enough youth workers, in a good enough youth ministry, the teenagers we serve will find themselves on a wonderful trajectory of spiritual growth, getting a little closer to Jesus every day.

But if you've worked with teens for any amount of time (literally, ANY amount of time spent with teenagers will teach you this), you've discovered that the picture above simply isn't realistic. After all, it's not realistic for you and me, so why would it be a realistic picture of faith development for our teenagers?

A more realistic picture, one most of us would agree with, looks more like this.

The teenage journey isn't clean, and every day doesn't result in new steps of growth. Instead it's a journey of highs and lows, peaks and valleys. You may even liken it to the stock market; it's a long-term investment that, despite setbacks, experiences growth over time. This picture makes sense because it's the picture we've all been taught over the years concerning spiritual growth.

But I'd like to suggest a third picture.

EMBRACE THE SQUIGGLE

This is the journey every teenager in your youth group finds themselves on. For an adolescent, life isn't as clean and tidy as the first two pictures suggest. Even the second picture with its peaks and valleys communicates a sense of predictability and normalcy. But the only normal thing most teenagers experience is that there is almost nothing normal about their lives! Life for a teenager is a messy, confusing, squiggly journey.

Over the course of my youth ministry career, I've had the joy of writing a few books and traveling upon occasion to train and encourage other youth workers. The concept of embracing the squiggle may end up being my biggest contribution to the cause of youth ministry (I'm not sure if that's a good or bad thing, actually). Every time I teach about it, I see "aha moments" on the faces of folks in the room. I've even used the squiggle to help parents understand why their teenagers are suddenly so frustrating. I hope you'll find it helpful, too. But please don't be like the youth worker who liked it SO much that he got an "Embrace the Squiggle" tattoo on his calf. That's a little weird. Maybe he has super bad short-term memory and didn't want to forget this simple concept as he headed into youth group each week.

But short of getting a tattoo, do what you need to do to remember the simple, but vital, practice of embracing the squiggle. Here are a few squiggle reminders:

3 BIGGIES IN A BOX

THE SQUIGGLE TAKES THE PRESSURE OFF
THE SQUIGGLE INVOLVES CHANGE, DOUBT, & INSECURITY
BECOME A SQUIGGLE ADVOCATE

The Squiggle Takes The Pressure Off
I love the squiggle because it reminds me that there are way more factors at play in ministry than merely my ability to be an awesome youth worker. If God expects me to keep the teenagers in my youth group on the straight trajectory of picture #1, I'm not

spiritual enough. If he demands that I provide a youth ministry that allows for some struggle but not much, like picture #2, I'm not smart enough. However, if God is handing me a bunch of teenagers who are already on a messy, squiggly journey and asks me to simply walk alongside them, nudging them toward him along the way...I'm his man; I can do that!

And that, my friends, is the picture of youth ministry. We can't fix every single student who walks through the doors of our church. We will never be good enough youth workers to ensure that no teenager under our care ever messes up. Embracing the squiggle is as much about the journey as it is about the destination. Embracing the squiggle is about choosing to journey alongside teenagers in their mess, in their confusion, in their doubts, and in their setbacks. Teenagers don't need adults who are trying to "straighten out" their journey (good luck with that, by the way). Instead they need adults who understand and embrace the squiggle, adults who are comfortable ministering in the mess.

And maybe that's all God really expects from us. Do you feel a little weight being lifted from your shoulders right now? That's the feeling of the Holy Spirit taking the pressure off!

The Squiggle Involves Change, Doubt, & Insecurity

CHANGE
If I could only use one word to describe the adolescent years, "change" would be the winner. Teenagers, especially younger ones, are going through a tremendous amount of change physically, emotionally, socially, intellectually, and spiritually. As a result, virtually every aspect of their lives is in flux, in one way or another. Their physical changes result in growth spurts, acne, and moving from "cute kid" to "awkward teenager." Their emotional changes suddenly bring on a whole host of feelings and emotional extremes they've never before dealt with. Social changes usher in a season of figuring out where they fit in and why. Childhood friends often get set aside for new ones, and peer

acceptance suddenly rules the day. The intellectual changes they are experiencing result in new capacities for critical thinking, problem solving, and question asking, all of which contribute to the spiritual changes so many teens experience. This includes asking tough questions about faith, having sincere doubts for the first time, and moving from a childlike faith inherited at birth to a faith of their own.

For many adults (especially parents), these changes are cause for concern. It can be scary to watch teenagers navigate this new season. If it's scary for adults to watch from a distance, just think about how scary it is for teenagers who are living it every waking moment! So here's my advice: Don't watch it from a distance. Don't put space between yourself and teenagers when they need you most. Walk with them through the changes and celebrate each change as normative and part of God's incredible design process for his most cherished creation. In order to embrace the squiggle, you must embrace change.

DOUBT

A moment ago I mentioned that a lot of the changes teenagers experience are causes for concern among parents and youth workers. Having worked with thousands of parents and youth workers over the years, and having raised two teenagers myself, I can say with a fair amount of certainty that few things are more frightening than when a teenager begins to doubt his or her faith. And it happens almost all the time. Thirteen-year-olds who always accepted "because the Bible says so" as a valid answer suddenly begin to doubt, wondering if what the Bible says is valid. High schoolers who have always held onto a sexual ethic that Mom, Dad, and the church promote suddenly question why the rest of culture seems to see things differently. I get why all of this is scary. We assume that when people begin to doubt certain aspects of their faith, other aspects soon follow. We likely have a fair amount of history on our side to support this assumption. After all, if a teenager doubts the validity of Scripture, it follows that they would then begin to doubt a whole lot of what has been taught using

Scripture as authority. Scary, right?

Yes. And awesome!

Here's the deal: A mature, unshakeable, hope-filled faith requires doubt. Doubt is what causes us to develop workable answers to tough questions; it's what forces us to wrestle with truths that make no sense on the surface. When teenagers doubt and wrestle with their faith, they usually come out on the other side holding onto it more tightly. As youth workers, we have a choice to make. We can try to minister in a way that prevents doubt and nips it in the bud the moment it begins—or we can minister in a way that recognizes doubt as a natural result of the squiggle and leverage it to our advantage by celebrating doubts, encouraging tough questions, and helping teenagers wrestle with the areas of faith that they find troubling.

INSECURITY

"Teenagers are so insecure!" bemoans the fifty-year-old youth worker in skinny jeans (dang it, I'm wearing skinny jeans as I type this). "Why are the junior high girls so boy-crazy?" wonders the twenty-something college student who has had five boyfriends since moving away from home. You and I are insecure—yet we wonder why teenagers, who are smack-dab in the middle of navigating the squiggle, are insecure, too? Insecurity and teenagers go hand in hand. Heck, LIFE and insecurity go hand in hand. You aren't going to change it, so embrace it and help teens navigate the feelings and challenges that come along with the insecurity that is a natural part of the squiggle years.

Become A Squiggle Advocate

The teenagers in your community and church desperately need adult advocates in their lives, men and women who are on their side. One way to describe being an advocate of teenagers and the squiggle is to quit loving them and start liking them. In a church, everybody loves the teenagers. "I love those crazy junior highers in the name of the Lord," the usher convinces himself. "Of course

KEEP JESUS AT THE CENTER

we love our youth…that's why we gave them their own room all the way back in the most remote part of the building," say the elders as they pat one another on the back for their generosity toward the church of the future. Everybody in your church loves teenagers. They have to, because they are good Christians, and good Christians love everybody. And they may well love them, but they very possibly don't like them. Loving is a mandate; liking is a choice. The teens in your youth group need adults who enjoy being around them, who enjoy helping them navigate the squiggle. They need advocates who like them, not loving church folk who tolerate them.

I married a high school cheerleader. She wasn't a high school cheerleader when I married her, but she was a cheerleader during her high school years (hopefully that was an unnecessary clarification!). I married a high school cheerleader who knows nothing about sports. Zero. Zip. Nada. She doesn't know the difference between an extra point and a three-pointer. I was teasing her about this recently and expressed my opinion that she was obviously an underachieving cheerleader due to her complete incompetence concerning literally anything sports-related. To which she replied, "Kurt, my job as a cheerleader wasn't to be an expert on sports. My job was to be an unrelenting source of encouragement to the student athletes."

Change a few words in that reply and I think you have the perfect job description for youth workers who want to be advocates for teenagers. "Our job is to be an unrelenting source of encouragement for teenagers." Mic drop, anyone? You, my friends, are cheerleaders. Teenagers need unrelenting encouragement, and we are just the people to provide it. You don't have to be an expert on all things teenager, just cheer them on with unrelenting zeal.

One of my favorite passages of Scripture is found in Ecclesiastes 4:12:

"A person standing alone can be attacked and defeated, but two can stand back-to-back and conquer. Three are even better, for a triple-braided cord is not easily broken."

No teenager should feel like she is standing alone. Every person in your youth group should know that there are some adults who have their back. The above passage is a great reminder of our vulnerability, and the importance of strong allies. You want to be an advocate for teenagers? You want to embrace the squiggle and walk alongside your youth group members? Have their backs: Look out for them, protect them, warn them of danger, and fight on their behalf.

Embracing the squiggle and being an advocate for teenagers doesn't mean there's no room in youth work to challenge teens; it's not an endorsement of low bars and low expectations. It isn't an excuse to dismiss inappropriate behavior or turn a blind eye to destructive decision making. When you choose to embrace the squiggle, you aren't committing to a laissez-faire mentality of discipleship. Embracing the squiggle is simply recognizing reality and determining to lovingly walk with young people and advocate for them as they navigate their teenage years.

THOUGHTS FROM A VOLUNTEER
by Patti Dempster

I like math: It's straightforward, and there's a right answer. I like to bake for a similar reason: You mix ingredients according to the recipe and you get a delicious result. Imagine my surprise when I started serving in junior high ministry. "Straightforward" is not a word that applies. Nevertheless I read every book I could about ministry. I attended every seminar, convention, and training I could find. I was ready to lead junior highers to Christ and have them live their lives following their Savior. I learned quickly, though, that junior high ministry is not black and white. There is no recipe for success. But I've learned

KEEP JESUS AT THE CENTER

that there is a secret to it that matters more than any formula.

Let me tell you about Joe. He was one of THOSE junior high boys. He was a part of our youth group as well as a student in the school on our church property. I saw him at our mid-week study and Sunday school as well as in my Bible class. He drove everyone crazy. Except for me. I didn't accept his poor choices and never let him get away with anything. He loved skateboarding and obscure music and hated school. Most adults assumed he would drop out or get kicked out of school and would end up in prison, or with a traveling circus. I was worried too. I spent a lot of detention time with him. But I would talk with him, and I would listen to him. I always reminded him I was praying for him, and he would laugh.

His family moved away when he was a sophomore in high school and I didn't hear from him for years. I continued to keep him in my prayers. Then one day I got a card in the mail. I thought the almost illegible handwriting was familiar, and I was shocked to see that it was from Joe. It read, "Hey Mrs. D. I want you to know I am doing good. I graduated from high school SHOCKER and then joined the Army. It has been a challenge but I love it. I think it's time to thank you. I have never forgotten our talks and even when I was in trouble, you made me feel good. I always knew you were praying for me and I wouldn't admit it, but I liked that. I am getting married and we are active in our church. I want you to know that. I am so glad you didn't write me off. Thank you, I won't ever forget."

The secret I've learned is that my most effective ministry is accomplished through heart and the Holy Spirit, trusting the Lord for the outcome no matter how things look along the way. I like math and baking but I love teenagers even more. I want them to know they are valued and heard, just as they are. If they can be confident in that, they can be confident in their relationship with me, and open to trust that what I share with them is true. The timing of results cannot be predicted but I treasure Joe's note as a reminder that my job is to serve in love, and the rest is up to the Lord.

HOW TO BE **THE BEST** VOLUNTEER YOUTH WORKER

Patti Dempster has been serving with junior highers for over twenty years. She splits her time between her crazy husband, teenagers, grandchildren, and everything Disney.

CHAPTER 3
IMPROVE YOUR SERVE

Thank you. And, I apologize that it's taken me this long to type those words! Thank you for sacrificing a little—more likely a lot—of your hard-to-find free time to minister to teenagers. Thank you for serving in an area of the church that is overlooked by most adults. Thank you for investing in young men and women during some of the most formative years of their entire lives.

If you are a volunteer, this book was written with you in mind! I'm incredibly thankful there are churches on the planet that can afford to pay folks to work with teenagers, but most can't. I'm encouraged by the number of seminaries and Christian universities that emphasize youth ministry by offering classes in this field, even entire degrees, but most youth workers haven't had that sort of formal training. Most youth workers are just like most of you: men and women with busy lives of their own, filled up with all the worries and responsibilities that come with being a good employee, boss, spouse, friend, son, daughter, mom, dad, etc. who, on top of everything else, have added "youth ministry volunteer" to their list. You are the backbone of youth ministry! Youth ministry in the local church and the communities in which it serves would chug along just fine without paid professionals like me, but it would come to a screeching halt if it weren't for volunteers who choose to serve for free.

Chances are we've never met, and I don't know the context in which you serve, but I'm gonna go out on a limb here and make an assumption about every single one of you. I assume you are serving well. I assume you are giving this volunteer youth worker thing a pretty good effort. And I assume you want to get a little bit better at it, which is one reason you're reading this book to begin with.

Now that I've spent three paragraphs patting you on the back (hey, you don't get a paycheck, so you might as well get a pat on the back from time to time!), let's get down to business. Unless you already happen to be the best volunteer youth worker in the history of the world, you have some room for improvement. How can you serve to the very best of your abilities? I'm glad you asked! Here are a few very simple but powerful ways to improve your serve:

3 BIGGIES IN A BOX
- BE YOURSELF
- HELP YOUR LEADER WIN
- FILL THE GAPS

Be Yourself

Remember, there's only one you. You are a one-of-a-kind, handcrafted masterpiece. God knitted you together in your mother's womb. All of humankind shares the same basic features and ingredients that make us human beings, but yours were put together in the amazingly awesome and unique way that makes you, you. The world doesn't need two of you—if it did, God would have structured reproduction, DNA, and all that stuff differently. And because there's only one of you, the world, and your youth group, need you to be the very best, most confident, and capable version of yourself possible. Avoid the temptation to try becoming somebody you aren't because if you succeed, you, the world around you, and your youth group lose out on the benefits only the REAL you has to offer!

The title of this chapter might suggest I grew up playing tennis. I didn't. I grew up playing Pop Warner football and was a pretty decent wide receiver. In fact, in eighth grade I set the league record for receptions. I peaked in eighth grade. The reason I peaked in eighth grade was largely due to what happened to me in ninth grade. On the very first day of practice during my freshman year, our coaches lined us all up and asked us to pretend we were running backs about to take a handoff. Out of forty or so football players, I somehow managed to be the ONLY guy who knew the proper way to place my hands and arms to receive a handoff. My coaches looked at each other, then proclaimed to the whole team, "Johnston is our running back!"

My strength wasn't in being a running back. My strength was in being a wide receiver, but I was never given that opportunity. Our team would have been more successful, and I would have had way more fun, if I had been allowed to play to my strengths. The same is true in youth ministry. You have strengths and skills that have been God-given or developed over time, and they will greatly benefit your youth group! You can't do it all. You can't play every position on your youth ministry team, so be yourself and play to your strengths. The youth group will be more successful, and you will have way more fun along the way!

Have you ever noticed how good humans are at comparing themselves to others? Even though almost nothing good ever comes of it, many of us find the urge to compare really tough to ignore. I'm convinced the comparison trap is one of the things that radically hinders youth workers. It keeps us from celebrating our uniqueness and playing to our strengths. If I'm always wishing I were more like the twenty-one-year-old volunteer who hangs out with seventh graders at the skate part, I'll underestimate the value I bring as a fifty-something-year-old who raised two kids in our youth ministry. If you constantly compare yourself to the stay-at-home mom who gives fifteen hours per week to the youth group, you will diminish the powerful impact you're making in your two hours per week as a small group leader!

Remember, there's only one you. So be yourself, play to your strengths, and avoid comparing how your unique contribution measures up to the contributions of others. Simply being yourself is a vital first step to improving your serve.

Help Your Leader Win

You may be one of several dozen volunteers serving in a large youth ministry under the leadership of a full-time youth ministry professional. Or, you may be one of a handful who help the bi-vocational youth minister make the best use of her time. Perhaps your youth ministry team is made up entirely of volunteers with nobody being paid to lead the way. Whatever the case, somebody is in charge and you can improve your serve by helping that person win. The best place to start? I'd suggest you start by giving the leader of your youth group what they need the most: prayer, and lots of it! Put his name at the top of your prayer list. Set a reminder on your phone and pray for her at the same time every day. Call the senior adults who head up your church's prayer chain and ask them to add your youth pastor's name. Every now and then, one of the volunteers on our youth team will shoot me a text or pull me aside at church simply to remind me that they are praying for me. I'm telling you, that NEVER gets old! When I know the volunteers on my team are lifting me up in prayer, I feel more comfortable as their leader and more confident in leading the way. My hunch is whoever leads your youth group would feel the same way.

Another way to help the leader of your ministry win is to commit to "Praise in public and punch in private." We all know how incredibly powerful public affirmation can be, and how damaging public criticism is. When you affirm a leader in front of others, three great things happen: She gains confidence in herself, others gain confidence in her, and she views you as a trusted ally. When you reprimand a leader in public, three unfortunate things happen: He loses confidence in himself, others lose confidence in him, and he views you as an untrustworthy opponent. This doesn't mean there's no place for criticism or holding our leaders accountable; in fact I'd argue that it probably doesn't happen enough. But there's a time and a place, and the best place to give your leader a "gut punch" is someplace private. A well-timed, private word of correction or concern is part of your role as a member of the youth ministry team, and if you've taken the occasional opportunity to praise him in public, your youth pastor will trust you and your motives when you feel compelled to "punch" him in private. (Note: Punch in private, but never punch the privates.)

Finally, you can help the leader win by minimizing surprises. I had only been on staff at Saddleback Church for a couple of weeks when the unthinkable happened: I left a teenager at the arena after taking our youth group to a major sporting event. This is the first time I've admitted publicly that it was my fault; for over twenty years I've blamed my friend and coworker, Katie Edwards, for miscounting. But the truth is it was on me. (That feels shockingly freeing to admit!) The worst part of the story is that we had NO idea we had left the young man behind until we were met at church by his angry dad. Mom was on her way to the arena to get their son, and Dad wanted a pound of my flesh. Eventually cooler heads prevailed, and I headed home with my teeth intact but my confidence shattered. I decided to call my supervisor right away so that he wouldn't be caught off guard by the news that would certainly find its way to him sooner or later.

Sure, part of the reason I gave him a heads up was to cover my own butt, but the bigger reason was that I valued him as a leader and wanted to protect him from being surprised. I hoped to give him plenty of time to formulate a thoughtful response to a set of parents who were rightfully frustrated. I wanted him to exude calm, confidence, and clear thinking in the moment, which wouldn't happen as easily if "in the moment" happened to be the first time he'd heard about the incident.

Minimize mistakes. You can start by being better at counting heads than I am. And when things go wrong, be sure to help your

Fill The Gaps

Perhaps the best way to improve your serve and increase your value to the team is to fill the gaps. Every ministry has gaps, and so does every leader. One of the best ways to improve your serve is to identify what ministry and leadership gaps you can offset by playing to your strengths. Instead of complaining that the youth leader isn't well organized, offset those weaknesses with your incredible organizational skills. When it's obvious the youth pastor doesn't do well in crisis, offset those weaknesses with your ability to stay cool under pressure. She's a poor communicator? Put your teaching credential to use in Sunday school! He's easily frustrated? Volunteer to take over the sixth grade small group for him! I have very poor bedside manner; confidently ministering to teenagers and families in times of their deepest pain is a massive gap in my leadership and pastoral skills. Praise the Lord there are a few volunteers in our youth ministry who excel at it; I try to take one of them with me every time I have to stumble and bumble my way through a tough pastoral moment. Offsetting your leader's weaknesses is a trifecta of wins: You win because you are playing to your strengths, your leader wins because he gets to watch you in action (and maybe learn a thing or two), and the youth group wins because better ministry is happening as a result!

It's easy to see a gap in the youth ministry and assume that the leader is aware of it and well on her way to correcting the situation. It's natural to wait to be asked to do something rather than just doing it. But if you want to improve your serve, both of those postures are mistakes. Whether they know it or not, your youth leader needs you to take initiative—to see a problem and solve it, to notice a gap and fill it. There's an old saying that goes something like "It's easier to put a fire out than to start one." I happen to know for a fact that is not a literal truth because in sixth grade I accidently, and easily, set my friend's kitchen on fire. It wasn't so easy to put out. That saying, though, is a leadership proverb: It's addressing the truth that when it comes to working with people, it's easier to slow down an overachiever than it is to light a fire under a sloth. Unless your youth pastor is incredibly insecure (and that's certainly not outside the realm of possibility), he wants you to take initiative! Sure, she may have to slow you down from time to time and remind you that while she is incredibly thankful you took the initiative to do so, painting the rusty old church bus hot pink wasn't necessary. But guess what? That night in bed, she will thank the good Lord she has volunteers on her team who notice gaps and take the initiative to fill them. Then she'll ask you to repaint the bus.

One of the best ways to fill the gaps in your youth ministry is to pay attention to where things are headed. NHL Hall of Famer Wayne Gretzky was asked what separated him from other players and his answer was fascinatingly obvious: "I skate to where the puck is going to be, not to where it has been." Wayne Gretzky would get to where the puck was headed before it ever arrived. I think his words of wisdom are fantastic for youth workers everywhere. You can look at where your youth ministry has been and see all sorts of gaps, but filling them in after the fact is of limited value. Most youth workers are plenty capable of looking at where the ministry is right now and identifying the gaps. That's important stuff. But great youth workers—the best volunteer youth workers in the history of the world—are those rare men and women who pay attention to where the youth group is headed, identify the gaps, and fill them before the ministry ever arrives.

THOUGHTS FROM A VOLUNTEER
by Gary Eilts

It's unlikely I'd be picked out of a lineup as the student ministries volunteer. I got into the game late, at thirty-six, and I'm now sixty-six years old. I embraced my call to junior high ministry in late 1989 as God's will "for a season."

At the time I was a single dad with an eight-year-old daughter and had no experience working with or communicating with teenagers.

The notion of leaning into who God has made me to be and trusting that is enough has served me well. It's now taken me through years of serving under seven different junior high pastors at my church. To piggyback on Kurt's football story, there were many times, especially early on, when I was asked to carry the ball in some fashion. Often, and especially over the last ten years or so, I've purposefully sought out opportunities to fill in the gaps: pinch-hitting, setting screens, coaching, and blocking (so to speak) for those tasked with carrying the ball for our ministry.

Each new pastor has had unique strengths and has required support in different ways; the gaps are ever-changing. Being available and being flexible have allowed me to adjust my game to complement their leadership while recognizing my evolving life circumstances as a thirty-, forty-, fifty- and sixty-something volunteer. As things have changed in the ministry and in my own life, I've shifted gears up and down accordingly.

A lot has happened in thirty years. I remarried and have had four daughters in our blended family (currently ages fifteen to thirty-eight) come up through our junior high ministry. Fun fact: I met my wife of twenty-one years while we were both serving as volunteers at our junior high ministry's winter camp in 1998. (Is that ministry with benefits?) Balancing family, work, and volunteering over several decades has of course presented challenges. I've found that staying confident that God has put me here to serve tweens and teens and my church by being myself has allowed me to be used in a variety of ways through all of the shifts and changes. If at any point I had tried to be less myself and more like the twenty-year-old volunteer hanging out with seventh graders at the skate park, my ministry would have been frustrating and short-lived.

IMPROVE YOUR SERVE

I'm now a grandpa! I don't play videogames or use TikTok or Snapchat. I can't really dodge a ball anymore. But I love junior highers, I love serving alongside my wife, and I am proud to share that our eighteen-year-old and twenty-five-year-old daughters are also now serving in junior high ministry. Your journey probably won't look like mine, but YOU BE YOU and God will use you in ways you could never have imagined.

Gary Eilts has been a junior high volunteer for over thirty years. He is married with four daughters and two grandkids. Gary is semiretired from a forty-year career in direct mail advertising.

HOW TO BE **THE BEST** VOLUNTEER YOUTH WORKER

CHAPTER 4
BE A TEAM PLAYER

Google the word "teamwork" and you'll discover that it is defined in a variety of ways, each similar but with slight nuances. I mashed a bunch of them together and came up with my own definition: "The combined action of a group of people working toward a common goal, especially when effective and efficient." Using this definition, we can make three interesting assumptions. First, teamwork can't happen if only one person is involved; it requires a group effort. Second, if there's no common goal there's no real teamwork. And third, just because there is a group working together toward a common goal doesn't ensure teamwork is present; effectiveness and efficiency help determine if the group effort is, in fact, teamwork.

I'll be the first to admit that "effective and efficient" isn't a phrase that gets me excited about youth ministry. It doesn't make for a very exciting recruitment pitch in the church bulletin—unless your ideal youth ministry volunteer is an accountant. I define effective as doing the right things, and efficient as doing things the right way, so I think it's fair (although admittedly unsexy) to say that the goal of a youth ministry team should be to work together in an effective and efficient manner.

So, what are the right things, and what's the right way to do them? Well, that's for the leadership of your youth group to determine.

There are lots of ways to do good, healthy youth ministry, lots of right things your ministry can do, and lots of right ways to do those things. That's the beauty of the kingdom of God: There is very rarely one perfectly-prescribed approach to the tasks at hand. But we do know that God seems to prefer a team approach to kingdom work. He has designed the body of Christ to work together in a way that is both effective and efficient. In God's kingdom, teamwork makes the dream work!

But teamwork doesn't come easily. Gathering a group of people committed to working toward a common goal in an effective and efficient manner is WAY tougher than it sounds. And while it's ultimately the responsibility of the person charged with leading your youth group, his or her ability to build a healthy team and, ultimately, a healthy youth ministry depends largely on you and the other members of the team.

So let's look at a few things you can do to help make teamwork a reality in your setting:

BIGGIES IN A BOX
PULL ON THE SAME SIDE OF THE ROPE
COMMIT TO TWO COMMITMENTS
KILL THE THREE TEAM KILLERS

Pull On The Same Side Of The Rope

I'm not a big fan of Tug o' War. I'm old, I don't weigh very much, I'm weak, and I hate rope burns.

There have been seasons in my youth ministry career that felt like one big game of Tug o' War, where instead of working well together, our youth team was struggling to find our footing, pulling back and forth against each other.

A healthy youth ministry team determines to pull on the same side of the rope—especially on the areas of most importance.

BE A TEAM PLAYER

Obviously, a level of healthy disagreement and varying opinions add flavor and diversity to a team, but those things can't be allowed to impede everybody's commitment to pulling on the same side of the rope when it comes to the bigger picture.

Here are three of the key areas where pulling on the same side of the rope is important:

THEOLOGY

Do you know your church's theology concerning things like sexuality, gifts of the Spirit, eternal security, the role of leadership, etc.? While theology may not be all that important to you, it is important to most churches. Theological differences are why there are literally hundreds of Protestant denominations (that and a thirst for power among leaders, but I digress). And while you certainly don't need to agree with every single theological position your church holds, you do need to know what it views as most important and be willing to adhere to what's on that list while you serve under its roof. Ninety percent of the time this isn't a big deal, but start speaking in tongues during a Baptist church's ninth grade Sunday school or begin whispering about "once saved, always saved" while serving in an Assemblies of God setting and you'll quickly see my point. Neither behavior is inherently wrong, but in certain settings they can be seen as pulling on the wrong side of the rope and hindering teamwork.

STRATEGY

Every youth group has a strategy. It may be clearly stated and regularly articulated, it may be an unwritten approach to youth ministry that is woven into the fabric of your church's DNA, or it may be like the mercies of the Lord—new every morning. In some settings, the point person determines the strategy, and in others the vision and direction are created by the entire team. Whatever the case, teamwork can only happen when people are on board with the current strategy and pulling on the same side of the rope to see that strategy implemented. By no means does this imply that the strategy and direction of the youth group are meant to be dictates set in stone, handed down from on high never to be questioned or evaluated. It simply means that whatever happens to be the current vision for healthy youth ministry in your setting, you need to help make it become a reality!

RULES AND REGULATIONS
I started working with teenagers in the local church setting in 1988. Back then, it was considered good clean fun to snap kids with towels at camp, to stick them to the wall with duct tape, and to "swirl" the occasional twelfth-grade head in the toilet. I can clearly remember being patted on the back by my supervisor for delivering fifteen junior highers to our Friday morning prayer gathering despite the fact that I drove a Volkswagen van with seating and seatbelts for seven. Things that were a regular part of youth group thirty years ago would get you fired today, and rightfully so! Hopefully your church has some guidelines in place to help ensure what it considers appropriate, encouraging, and healthy youth ministry. Some of guidelines are mandated by law, some are mandated by the church's insurance provider, and a whole bunch are mandated by the church leadership, possibly including things that might not be concerning in another church setting. Please play by the rules. Please don't do stupid stuff. Please don't put the safety of teenagers at risk. Please don't do anything that causes emotional harm. Please don't put your church's financial security and reputation in the community in jeopardy. An entire team pulling on the same side of the rope is easily offset by one person who decides the rules and regulations don't apply to him.

Commit To Two Commitments
While building a team, no leader has ever said to herself, "I need to fill this team with as many flaky, untrustworthy people as I can find." Just the opposite! Every leader wants a team full of men and women who are trustworthy and committed to the cause. You could make the argument that Jesus's early disciples were a bunch of knuckleheads, but they were (mostly) trustworthy and committed to the cause, and the world was changed as a result.

BE A TEAM PLAYER

Two commitments every member of every great youth ministry team makes are:

- **Commit To What You've Committed To**
  Our youth ministry team has a saying: "Commit to what you've committed to." It's impossible to be committed to every single aspect of your youth ministry, and unhealthy to try. So instead of creating an "all or nothing" culture with our volunteers, we've simply created an atmosphere that allows volunteers to commit at whatever level they want, expecting them to be faithful to whatever that happens to be. If nobody's ever said this to you, let me be the first: You don't have to do everything. In fact, you can't do everything! You don't need to pull on the rope harder than everybody else; just pull your own weight. As the leader of our ministry, I can't remember ever being frustrated with a teammate who was committed to only a couple of areas of ministry, but I can tell you all sorts of stories about being frustrated with folks who were under-committed to tons of areas! Sure, their intentions were great—and so was the level of frustration they caused the rest of the team.

- **Commit To Maintaining Trust**
  In his best-selling book *The Five Dysfunctions of a Team*[1], Patrick Lencioni unearths the number one thing that hurts teamwork: a lack of trust. A team of people who trust one another, trust the leadership, trust the vision, and trust the strategy that will bring the vision to life is a team well on its way! When trust in any of these areas is broken, especially trust in each other, teamwork is jeopardized. Trust is hard to quantify, but you know it when you see it and you know when it's absent. In my experience, there are a few things that contribute to an atmosphere of trust on a youth ministry team:

  Honesty: Being honest with our concerns, frustrations, and shortcomings is a big piece of maintaining trust. A team functions best when teammates view each other as honest.

Safety: Unfortunately, many teams are honest at the expense of being safe. On our teams, people need to be able to share a bad idea without being shamed or express an honest concern without being labeled as a rebel or someone who isn't on board with the vision. Your team needs to be a safe place for leaders to disagree, make mistakes, and fall short.

Consistency: This ties into the idea of being committed to what you've committed to. If you are consistent and can be counted on by the rest of the team, they'll trust you.

Kill The Three Team-Killers

Okay, you are part of a youth ministry team full of trustworthy men and women who are committed to the cause. Fantastic! Your team is well on its way to world-class awesomeness. But danger lurks around every corner. Lots of things can derail a healthy team if you take your eye off the ball. Here are three team-killers you need to help kill. But beware, these are zombie-like: Just because you think you've dealt with them doesn't ensure they won't rise up when you least expect it and bite you in the neck.

- **Comparing**
  Rarely does anything good come from comparing. Avoid the temptation to compare your level of commitment and passion to that of others on the team. Don't make the mistake of comparing your youth ministry appreciation party, held in the youth pastor's garage, with the bulletin-stuffers' appreciation party, held on a luxury yacht in the Bahamas. Not everything in the world of church volunteerism is fair. If you allow yourself to insist it should be, you are actually hurting your team, even if you feel like you are advocating on its behalf. Here's why: Comparing almost always leads to the next team-killer.

BE A TEAM PLAYER

- **Complaining**
  When you compare, the natural tendency is to focus on the areas where your ministry is falling short, and even the best-run youth ministries have room to improve. If you choose to, you can always find something to complain about. Camp is too expensive, the youth room is messy, the lesson plan didn't work, the youth director is unorganized, the church down the street has a bigger budget and nicer church van, and the other people on our team aren't pulling on the same side of the rope. Very few things hurt team morale as much as complaining, and if you are known as somebody who is never satisfied and who constantly focuses on the problems instead of the solutions, you will be a drain on the team and the ministry. Force yourself to be positive! Frame negative situations in a positive manner! I'm not suggesting you ignore the shortcomings and struggles in your ministry setting, I'm simply saying that if an atmosphere of complaining and negativity is allowed to take root in your team, dysfunction is soon to follow.

- **Cynicism**
  I played high school football on a not-very-good high school team. I was an average player on a below-average team. Good times. There were all sorts of reasons our team struggled to make good things happen on the field. We were consistently outsized, outcoached, and outplayed—which added up to being outscored on a weekly basis. But I'm not convinced those are the things that doomed us. In our senior season, two or three of our very best players came into "Hell Week" (that's the universal term for the first week of practice, which includes two practices a day, lots of wind sprints, and lots of pain) with a different attitude, and it wasn't a good one. From day one they questioned the coaches' decision making, they pointed out the flaws and faults of virtually everybody on the team, and they began predicting finishing the season 0-10. The only word to describe their attitude was one of cynicism. Cynicism is different from comparing and

complaining. While those qualities have a tendency to come and go depending on the circumstance, cynicism usually takes root. It takes up permanent residence in our hearts despite the circumstances. My teammates' cynicism doomed our season because it took root in their hearts. Even when we would miraculously find ourselves ahead in a game, in the huddle our best players would say things like, "Well, it's only a matter of time until they take the lead." When cynicism takes hold, it's almost impossible to break free. A cynical youth ministry volunteer will be like a boulder tied around everybody else's necks, dragging the entire team down. A cynical teammate can question every decision, assume the worst in every situation, and sow division instead of helping to build unity.

I'm not much of a fighter. Probably because in eighth grade I got beat up by a seventh grader. Don't judge me—she was tough! But I'll fight for a healthy youth ministry team and I hope you will, too! Fight the temptation to compare and complain because cynicism is lurking just around the corner—kinda like a seventh-grade girl. A tough seventh-grade girl.

THOUGHTS FROM A VOLUNTEER
by Billy Hinzo

After a group of boys I'd been leading for four years graduated from high school—and after what had been my toughest season in youth ministry (and my career) to date—I was ready to take a break. The group had split in their junior year. I lost my job around the same time and had limped to the finish line. I didn't volunteer for summer camp that year. I was focused on growing a new company and was starting to wonder if this was the end of my involvement in youth ministry.

That's when I got the call from one of the youth workers on staff

BE A TEAM PLAYER

at my church. "Billy, I need you to pray about taking one for the team," he said. He explained that there was a group on the verge of abandoning their small group leader. These boys had been in the same class in Christian school every year since kindergarten and held a fair amount of student leadership roles within the ministry. This core group of kids had a brand-new small group leader, Freddy, who loved the Lord but was extremely new to his faith.

After his coleader moved to Los Angeles mid-year, Freddy had been thrown into the role of singlehandedly leading these guys in his first year of ministry. There was a good number of parents and teenagers who felt they deserved a "seasoned" or "dope" leader (depending on whether you asked a parent or a high schooler) with in-depth Bible knowledge, someone who'd be able to provide a challenging environment. I was asked to pray about coleading the group, providing the bastion of youth ministry experience they were looking for before they'd agree to stick it out.

Despite feeling low on fuel, I met with Freddy and knew God was calling me to this. I immediately felt this young leader's brimming love for serving and discipling these guys, despite their initial rejection of him. I could tell he was a team player who wasn't concerned with being the most popular, but rather wanted to set ego aside and do whatever was necessary to create a group environment where we pursued Jesus.

What came next was a beautiful display of pulling on the same side of the rope. While I may have symbolized a life raft to people on the outside, I knew that on the inside I didn't have the energy to keep this crew afloat. We each contributed as we were able. I encouraged Freddy to keep leading the majority of the conversations during our lessons and to keep planning our gatherings. Meanwhile I cherry-picked some relational ministry opportunities from within the larger group, connecting with high schoolers in smaller groups and one-on-one. Initially, the guys were super pumped to have a vetted leader join in with them, but Freddy was the one who provided integral leadership during the remaining three years the group met together.

Along the way, Freddy and I were honest with each other about what we were each able to bring to the table. We learned to trust that one would prop up the other when needed. Rather than Freddy trying to double down on convincing the guys he was a super-leader, or me trying to dunk on Freddy for being new, we committed to tackling each situation together. Early on Freddy may have felt he couldn't have done it without me, but I certainly couldn't have led this group without him.

Fast forward to today: We're both small group coaches within the ministry and now pour into leaders who are just starting out (like Freddy once was) or who are on the verge of burnout (like I once was). Next time you feel like a challenge requires more output than you can handle, look around and see if you can get everyone pulling on the same side of the rope. The once immovable mountain may very well start moving.

Billy Hinzo has been a volunteer youth worker with high school students for ten years. Aside from youth ministry, he owns and operates Kingdom Nutrition Inc. based out of Rancho Santa Margarita, CA.

CHAPTER 5
HELP PARENTS WIN

Youth ministry and parents have a long history: As long as there has been youth ministry, there have been parents (profound stuff, that!). If the relationship between youth ministry and parents were a book, I think we would be in the middle of chapter two. Let me explain.

Chapter one could have lots of names, all meaning basically the same thing: "Parents, You Stick to Parenting and Let Us Do the Heavy Spiritual Lifting," or "Parental Influence vs. Youth Group Influence," or "Hey Parents, You Mess Them Up But We're Here to Fix Them," or "Parents, Get Out of the Way and Let the Youth Group Save the Day." The mentality in chapter one was basically that it was best to keep parents, and their various roles, mostly separate from the various roles of a youth group. As the "profession" of youth ministry gained more popularity and churches across the country hired more qualified youth pastors and provided more and more resources to the youth ministry, some of the roles that parents traditionally provided began to shift to the youth group. It was all well-intentioned. Middle-aged parents of teenagers struggling to raise their children saw allies in the youth group full of younger, cooler followers of Jesus their children related to and respected. That was fine—until it wasn't. Pretty soon, parents began to assume the church was better equipped to disciple their children than they were, and most youth workers assumed the same thing. Before long the assumption among most Christian parents and the church was that since parents were ill-equipped and struggling in their role, the church would offer an amazing youth group that would provide great leaders as spiritual stepparents and amazing programs to keep the teenagers out of trouble and on the right path. In my limited understanding of recent church and youth ministry history, this had two unfortunate results:

1. It shifted the primary responsibility of helping teenagers follow Jesus from the parents to the youth group.
2. As a result, it minimized the importance of the role of parents in the lives of their teenagers and allowed many youth ministries to, at best, view parents as mostly unnecessary. At worst it pitted the influence of the youth group against the influence of mom and dad.

Enter chapter two, which I think would best be titled, "Let's Help Parents Win!!" Chapter two is a direct reaction to chapter one and reflects all the lessons we've learned over the years. Parents aren't the enemy, parents have the very best of intentions, parents truly are the most important influence in the lives of their teenagers, the youth group doesn't hold all the answers and certainly shouldn't be viewed in higher esteem than mom and dad. In chapter two, we are recognizing the incredible value of partnering with parents, ministering to parents and helping them win in their efforts to raise their kids. In chapter two, we are figuring out ways the youth group can fill some of the gaps here and there without undermining parents' influence or doing the heavy spiritual lifting on their behalf. There is still a MASSIVE need for good youth groups (whew!), but the very best youth groups out there are the ones making a concerted and strategic effort to serve parents, helping set the stage for their success.

You're reading this little book because you are a volunteer youth worker, well on your way to becoming the best volunteer youth worker in the history of the world. You don't have enough hours in

HELP PARENTS WIN

your volunteer week to focus all of your efforts on ministering to parents, nor should you. The bulk of partnering and ministering to parents should be done by whoever is the point-person tasked with carrying the leadership of the entire youth ministry. The ways you can serve parents might be limited, but they are important nonetheless. Here are three ways the best volunteer youth worker in the history of the world can help parents win:

3 BIGGIES IN A BOX

EARN THEIR TRUST
ESTEEM THEIR ROLE
ENCOURAGE THEIR INVOLVEMENT

Earn Their Trust

Your relationship with parents begins and ends with trust. In our ministry, we like to say "If parents are for us, who can be against us!?" When parents trust you, it opens up all sorts of significant opportunities to partner with them that go far beyond loaning you their SUV or opening their home to a midweek small group gathering (although they won't do that stuff either if they don't trust you). I've learned that trust with parents is largely earned in the littlest of things. Good communication, advance planning, not automatically believing that their child's side of the story is the most accurate side, and creating a safe environment are just a few relatively simple things you can do to help earn the trust of parents. When parents trust you they'll invite your input, ask for your guidance, and view you as an important ally as they raise their teenagers.

Esteem Their Role

Helping parents win means working with them, not against them. It means recognizing the incredibly important role they play in the lives of their teenagers, even though that role is beginning to change. One of the quickest ways for a volunteer to land in hot water with our leadership team is if they undermine, undercut, or undervalue the role of moms and dads. Parents are overwhelmed, and oftentimes feel underequipped for the teenage years. They're insecure and afraid. One of the best ways we can help them win is by consistently valuing and esteeming their role. How? A few simple examples:

- **Don't Pile On**
  When a student is complaining about mom or dad, don't add fuel to their fire! Instead of saying, "Yeah, I've noticed your parents still treat you like a little kid!" look for a way to esteem mom and dad by saying, "I bet it's pretty scary being the parent of a teenager. Even though you are getting older they still want to protect you. I understand why that feels awkward to you. Have you been able to talk to them about it?"

- **Don't Put a Wedge in the Relationship**
  This is a tough one because every family has its own unique rules, values, expectations, worldview, etc. So do you. So does your youth group. And sometimes when those things collide, you inadvertently (I know you would NEVER do so on purpose) put a wedge between parents and their kids. It can be in the littlest of ways, such as inviting all the seventh-grade boys to a PG-13 movie, not taking into account that a few families may have house rules against such movies until their kids are older. You've put mom and dad in the position of either being the bad guys and not allowing their son to go to the movie with the rest of the group, or bending their values so their son doesn't feel left out. You can put a wedge between parents and teenagers when you sarcastically roll your eyes in agreement when an eleventh-grade girl is complaining that her parents don't approve of her choice in a boyfriend. If parents begin to feel like you are a source of friction in their relationship with their teenager, their trust will quickly erode.

- **Constantly Speak Highly of Them**
  Because teenagers know everything, and because moms and dads don't have a clue about literally anything, it's natural that the teens in your youth group feel safe venting to you about their various grievances. And they should. At the same time, parents should be able to trust that whenever possible, you will look for ways to esteem them and speak highly of them.

Encourage Their Involvement

Not long ago it was commonplace in many youth groups to have a formal rule stating that parents were not allowed to volunteer in the ministry. The main reasoning was that teenagers needed a safe place to get away from it all. The thought was that they wouldn't be as honest and open during discussion times if parents were in the room. Fair enough. There were certainly other reasons for this rule that weren't explained explicitly, such as beliefs that parents are kill-joys, overly critical, and they will cramp our style. Not quite so fair. But times have changed, and most youth groups now recognize how incredibly valuable parents can be to a thriving, healthy, youth group! Parents are a little older and wiser than most youth leaders, parents are living with teenagers 24/7 and have their "boots on the ground" in real time, and parent volunteers add credibility and trust with other parents. Sure, you need to be thoughtful about how a parent's involvement feels to their child and what parental involvement in your ministry looks like. You don't have to allow every parent who wants to be involved to do so, just like you don't have to allow every random adult who wants to be involved to do so.

In our ministry we have three questions we ask parents before allowing them to serve:

1. How does your child feel about it? A reluctant teenager isn't a deal-breaker, but you need to make sure a real conversation between them has happened.

2. Do you want to minister to ALL teenagers, or just your own? It's important that parents who serve have a heart for youth ministry as a whole, versus simply viewing it as a way to spend quality time with their own child.

3. Is your interest in volunteering due to any sort of lack of trust? Do you mostly want to serve because you don't trust your child and want to keep an eye on him? Do you want to serve because you don't trust this ministry and want to keep an eye on us?

Help parents win. It takes work, but there's really no other option if you want to be the best volunteer youth worker in the history of the world!

THOUGHTS FROM A VOLUNTEER
by Tom Wheeler

As a junior high volunteer, I get to directly influence teenagers for maybe two to four hours a week. And those hours are usually split between a number of teens at one time. Parents spend so much more time with their kids and have many more opportunities to influence them. By aligning myself with parents and helping them be successful at home, I can leverage my time spent with teenagers and influence them more effectively.

Helping parents win begins with building a positive relationship based on things like good communication, being on time, acting trustworthy, and looking out for the interests of both parents and teens. All these actions result in building trust. Of course, the best way to build trust with parents is to be genuinely interested in their child.

I help lead a small group of junior high boys. One of the first things I like to do with a new group is have a dinner at a local food court with both the boys and the parents. Inevitably, the boys eat fast and start running around, which gives me time to connect with their moms and dads. Each parent has their own story about their junior higher that includes family dynamics, hopes, and concerns. I try to hear each family's story. I ask open-ended questions.

Throughout the year, I send out an email once a week with the basic facts of where we are meeting, what time, and, most importantly, who is in charge of this week's snack. If I remember to, I'll send a photo or a highlight of what we are studying so parents can follow up if they like. If parents can count on you to communicate, be somewhat organized, and be on time, it makes it easier for them to support your activities as a group.

One of the important roles I play as a small group leader is to help bridge the gap between teenagers and their parents. Teenagers need a safe place to share about their lives, and maintaining confidentiality is important to building trust with your teens. But as they share, it gives you a unique opportunity to encourage them to share these same things with their parents. Some of these kids are walking through deep struggles where it would be helpful, and sometimes essential, for a parent to know what is going on. In these instances, I try to get the junior higher to share with his mom or dad.

Bridging the gap can also be as simple as encouraging parents. It's helpful to remind them of the good you see in their kid and that what they are going through is fairly normal for this time of their kid's life. Encourage parents to show interest in their teen's life by asking open-ended questions. Supporting them helps give moms and dads the confidence and thick skin required to parent teenagers.

I've found that although they may have a strong exterior, most kids just need to be nudged to talk with their parents. As a volunteer for junior high boys, I've learned that it's extremely important to encourage teenagers to develop relationships at home to support them and their spiritual growth.

Tom Wheeler has been a volunteer youth worker with junior highers for six years. When not spending time with teenagers, he is a Public Works Director and City Engineer in Southern California.

CHAPTER 6
BE INTERESTED, NOT INTERESTING

Recently I was tag-team preaching with my senior pastor in the adult worship service. He was preaching away, and I was sitting in the wings frantically reviewing my notes. I'm not normally frantically reviewing my notes minutes before I head to the stage, but because I had been told a mere twenty-four hours earlier that I was going to help out, and because my portion of the sermon had been changed twice in that short timeframe, I wasn't totally confident in WHAT I was supposed to teach, let alone HOW I was gonna preach it. The message was on friendship. I had no idea what my pastor was saying, what verses he was quoting, or what I was actually going to add to the topic. I was in a full-blown panic mode. The only thing I can remember my pastor saying during his part of the sermon was this gold nugget of friendship wisdom:

"If you want to be a good friend…be interested, not interesting."

That's some solid friendship wisdom, and I think it's equally awesome advice for those of us who work with teenagers!

The teens in your youth group don't need you to be interesting. They don't need you to be cool. They don't need you to be charismatic. They don't need you to dress like them, talk like them, or be as social media savvy as they are. Quit trying to compete with the social media influencers they follow. You don't need to learn to drop into a bowl at the skate park. Heck, you don't even need to learn how to balance on a skateboard! You don't need to wow teenagers with your theological knowledge or philosophical musings.

Your teenagers are surrounded by interesting people but, sadly, probably know very few people who are genuinely interested in them. You want to gain influence in the life of a teenager? You want to earn the right to speak into their life? You want to be the kind of adult teenagers can't wait to spend time with? It's easier than you think: Be interested. Here are a few ideas:

3 BIGGIES IN A BOX

ASK GOOD QUESTIONS
LISTEN MORE THAN YOU SPEAK
BE INTERESTED IN WHAT INTERESTS THEM

Ask Good Questions

We've seen the same scene play out over and over again on the big and small screens. Boy and girl go out on a first date and things don't going very well. Why? "All she did was talk about herself all night." Or, "He just wouldn't quit talking…"

One of the very best ways to let teenagers know you are interested in them is to be someone who asks lots and lots of really good questions. Become a question-asking guru, the Yoda of questions. Asking good questions is an art, and you'll get better at it over time. Here are a few tips to give you a head start:

- **The Best Questions Are Open-ended**
  Instead of asking, "How was your week?" frame the question in a way that forces them to elaborate a little bit: "What was the best part of your week? What made it so good?"

- **Practice the Art of the Follow-Up Question**
  After you ask an amazing open-ended question, you will

probably be met with an equally amazing, five-minute response. (Or not.) During their response, pick out one or two things that can spur a follow-up question: "So…getting an A on your science test was the best part of your week. Did you do anything different to ensure such a great result, or do you always do so well?"

- **Ask "Wheelhouse" Questions**
  This tip works a whole lot better with students you know fairly well. Avoid asking questions a teenager will have a hard time answering. If you know your teens, you know which ones are great students and which ones struggle academically. You know who is an athlete and who isn't. Ask questions that fall into the wheelhouse of the teenager you are talking to. Ask sports questions of the athlete. Ask a question about SAT prep of the academic. But whatever you do…don't ask an athlete a question about SAT prep! (If you are offended, please email me at: Iwasjustjoking@someathletesaresmart.com.)

Listen More Than You Speak

This goes along with asking good questions: It's harder to listen if you never ask good questions and give teenagers something to talk about! But there's much more to it than that. I've discovered that a high percentage of adults who work with teenagers, 97.32% to be exact, actually do WAY too much talking. It makes sense. We've been around the block a few times. We've made a few mistakes, had a few successes, and learned a few lessons. We know Jesus and his Word. We have an established worldview that our teenagers would be wise to adopt. Why wouldn't we talk a lot? It's simple: Because talking doesn't show that you are interested, listening does.

Way back in the day I would hand my junior high volunteers a sticker to remind them of the importance of listening. It was a little drawing of a person with a tiny mouth and massive ears. When you listen more than you speak it sends a whole bunch of really important signals to your teens: "I'm here for you." "Your agenda matters more than mine." "I'm interested in what you have to say." "It's about you, not me."

Wayne Rice, junior high ministry guru and cofounder of Youth Specialties, is famous for saying, "Teenagers will gravitate toward the oldest person in the room who takes them seriously." You may not yet be fortunate enough to be the oldest person in the room, but you can be known as somebody who takes teenagers seriously. One of the best ways to do so is to listen more than you speak.

Be Interested In What Interests Them

Part of my role as the NextGen Pastor at my church includes ministering to parents, helping them win in their efforts to help their children become lifelong followers of Jesus. A common struggle parents have with their children, especially as they enter their teenage years, is a lack of shared interests. Mom is into cooking but her daughter is into sports. Dad loves to work on cars, but his son prefers to dive into a good book. When parents lament that they can't find a common interest, I always have the same response: "Be interested in what interests them!"

There is an urban legend in our youth ministry, one birthed about twenty years ago. When we train our leaders, we often refer to the legend of The Puzzle Technique for its wisdom about connecting with teenagers.

Julie was a veteran volunteer who was having trouble connecting with a girl who came each weekend, but always sat alone. One weekend, she asked a fairly basic open-ended question: "So, what are you into?"

"I like puzzles" was the short response. To which Julie, who was very adept at asking follow-up questions, replied, "Oh…what type of puzzles do you like?" The young teen gave a simple, one-word answer before she buried herself in her hoodie: "Jigsaw."
The following weekend Julie showed up to youth group with

hope in her heart and a jigsaw puzzle in her hands. She found her mark…and went in for the kill. The poor girl didn't stand a chance. How could she? Julie was an older, caring adult who knew how to listen, asked good follow-up questions, and took an interest in the thing that interested her young friend. And thus, The Puzzle Technique was born.

There's an old saying, widely attributed to Theodore Roosevelt, that church leaders have been quoting for years: "People don't care how much you know until they know how much you care." I think a paraphrase is equally accurate, especially when it comes to teenagers: "Teenagers don't care how interesting you are until they know how interested you are."

THOUGHTS FROM A VOLUNTEER
by Abby Edwards

It can be so easy to get caught up in trying to be the cool, fun, and favorite leader. We just want the teens in our ministries to love us, and we want them to hang out with us. I remember once telling some of my small group girls an embarrassing summer camp story thinking they would find it, and me, hilarious. I ended up embarrassing myself even more because when I finished the story instead of the reaction I expected, there were…crickets. Dead silence. In reality, teens don't need us to be super cool or tell amazing, hilarious stories. They just need leaders who will love them no matter what. They want us to ask good questions and listen to what they have been up to and care about what they are interested in.

I had one girl in my small group who loved anything and everything having to do with dragons. She was obsessed with a certain movie about dragons and had its corresponding merchandise, clothing, and books; she had even cut her hair so she would look like one of the movie's characters. True story. For

Christmas, she had received a book that talked about how the movie was made, the characters, and all the work that went into it. When we met at her house for small group she had the book out, so I did something very simple: I asked her about it. Her face completely lit up and she was more than happy to take me through it, page after page. It didn't matter whether I cared about the dragon movie. It mattered that I showed her that I cared what she cared about. That small moment made a deep impression on me and made a difference in building our relationship.

These are things teenagers will not forget. The important moments are the ones in which you truly listen, when you stop worrying about being interesting and start being interested. Occasionally, this means spending time talking about what has been going in their life and asking good questions. Other times, it means watching your small group members recreate TikTok videos for an hour or, of course, asking them about dragon movies. Teenagers don't really care if you're super interesting or have done really cool things. All they need is for you to listen, to ask about what is happening in their lives, and to love them no matter what. Doing that and teaching them about Jesus are the keys to being a great youth ministry volunteer.

Abby Edwards has been a volunteer youth worker with junior highers for three and a half years. When not spending time with teenagers, you can find her hanging out with her family or with a book in one hand and an iced coffee in the other.

CHAPTER 7
MASTER THE THREE KEY SKILLS

This chapter may seem a little out of place since the point of the entire book is helping you develop the skills you need to become the best volunteer youth worker in the history of the world. And while I think everything you've read so far is important, there are three skills that stand out from the rest and warrant some extra attention. These skills don't make for sexy book titles or draw large crowds to workshops, and I certainly never took a seminary class addressing them, but a case could be made that mastery of these skills sets a youth worker up for success—way more than the much sought-after youth ministry skills of being young, funny, athletic, and musically inclined. These skills are a natural part of some people's makeup and come very easily. Others have developed them through life experience. And for others, these skills will take a lifetime of intentional focus and practice. But whenever you master them…watch out! A youth group full of adult volunteers faithfully putting these skills into action will be virtually irresistible to teenagers. And here's the best part: These skills don't require a budget, or a nice youth room, or a seminary education. They aren't tied to the size of your church or its theology. These skills transcend gender, race, and social standing. Every adult volunteer can master them, and every youth group can benefit from them.

Consistency

Look, I know I said these skills aren't sexy, but I lied. There may not be a more attractive quality in a youth ministry volunteer than the willingness and determination to be consistent—to remain committed to what you've committed to. Consistency is a double-edged sword of awesomeness. When you are consistent, both the ministry and the teenagers who attend are direct beneficiaries.

I've been fortunate enough to serve at the same church since 1997, and during that time God has done some amazing things through our youth ministry. And while that statement is 100% true, it leaves out an important piece of reality. The whole truth is that God has done some amazing things through our youth ministry because of the volunteers who have consistently given up their time, talents, and treasures in service to the cause.

A lot of celebration and fuss are made over the volunteers who serve for long periods of time, and in our ministry we certainly make a big deal about celebrating our volunteers' ministry anniversaries after five, ten, fifteen, twenty, and twenty-five years. But I'll suggest that there's something more effective than longevity: consistency. I'd much rather have a volunteer who serves faithfully and consistently for a year than one who is flaky for five. Here are three significant results that await a consistent youth ministry volunteer:

- **Trust Is Built**
  The youth worker trusts you, teenagers trust you, parents trust you…it's a beautiful thing.
- **More Responsibility Is Given**

Being consistent in smaller areas almost always results in being given more leadership responsibility. Jesus taught about this reality from time to time.

- **Impact and Influence Are Increased**
  It's hard to make a positive impact in a ministry or in a relationship when you are inconsistent.

If youth ministry were an economy, consistency would be its currency.

Empathy

One way to describe empathy (to paraphrase the entry on Wikipedia) is the ability to understand and share the feelings of another from within their frame of reference.

Using that definition, it's hard to make a case that any quality is more important than empathy in an adult who is ministering alongside teenagers. Almost every teenager in your youth group is a mess in one way or another (embrace the squiggle!); it comes with the territory. Here's a short list of some of the things a typical teenager is navigating: friendships, social media, pressure to get good grades, peer pressure, anxiety, feeling alone, family issues, dating, first job, driver's license, bad hair days, fitting in... The list could go on and on. Add to all of this the fact that they are going through a tremendous amount of physical, social, intellectual, and emotional change as a natural part of their adolescent development, and you can see why being in close proximity to an empathetic adult is so important.

I'll be the first to admit that empathy doesn't come naturally to me. I grew up in a very poor, working class (mostly *not*-working class) family. The mantras my family lived by were "rub some dirt in it," "shake it off," "deal with it," "figure it out," and "toughen up." I entered adulthood, ministry, and marriage without knowing how to talk about my feelings, because nobody had ever asked me how I was feeling. I think that's why I like that the definition of empathy I used to open this section starts with the word "ability."

For some, it's a natural ability, but it's also an ability that can be learned! It's been a long learning curve for me but as I've grown in my ability to be empathetic, here are a few things that helped the journey.

- **Put Yourself in Their Shoes**
  Or more accurately, put yourself back into your own shoes. One of the best ways to empathize with a teenager is to go back in time and remember what it's like to be a teenager. If empathy requires sharing the feelings of others from within their frame of reference, then it means we can't try to see things from an adult perspective, but rather from that of a teenager. As adults we tend to forget what the teenage experience is like, and therefore we address their struggles, angst, and anxiety through our older, wiser eyes. Put yourself back into your teenage shoes. What were your fears? What was your relationship with your parents like? How did you see the world? How did you view Jesus? What temptations and sins did you struggle with?

  YES, your teenagers need an adult perspective…but they need you to share it while you wear your old teenage shoes.

- **Listen Without the Need To Fix**
  Providing quick, easy, pragmatic answers is never the right way to show empathy. Seeing the struggles teenagers are facing as projects on your checklist to correct before moving on might make sense to a forty-something business manager, but this will be borderline devastating to your relationships with the teens in your youth group. I'm learning the ability to be a good listener, and the more I listen without jumping into fix-it mode, the more my empathy grows.

- **Don't Fake It—Find Someone**
  You can't truly empathize with every teenager in every scenario. There will come a time when for one reason or another you simply can't share their feelings from their

perspective. It could be because of an innate bias you hold toward a particular scenario or because you've never experienced anything remotely close to what they are going through. That's okay! Don't fake it. Find somebody else on your team who is better equipped to empathize with that particular teenager. That's the beauty of the body of Christ: We all bring different experiences, skills, and gifts to the table. If you fake empathy (even if it's well-intentioned fakery), it is robbing that teenager of being ministered to by an adult who can truly empathize, AND it's robbing the other adult of the opportunity to put his or her life experience into action.

Grace

Like many, our church has a set of values that help guide the focus and emphasis of our various ministries. At the top of the list is something that I think might be the most important value, or skill, a youth worker can possess. The value at the top of our list says, Saddleback is a second chance grace place. I love that! Our church recognizes that life is full of hurts, habits, hang-ups, and heartache. Nobody is immune to needing second chances—especially not teenagers.

The teens in your youth group are going to disappoint others on a regular basis. They'll mess up, misstep, and misspeak. They'll gossip, goof off, and go off the rails. They'll cuss when they shouldn't, care less when they should care more, and commit all manner of wrongs. And when they do all of the above…over and over again…you will have the opportunity to give grace…over and over again. When your youth group is a second chance grace place led by second chance grace adults, it just might be the greatest youth group in the history of the world. Why? Because Jesus doesn't give a darn about cool games or great messages or fancy youth rooms. He's all about second chances (something about that whole "seventy times seven" mentality), and a youth ministry full of adults who are all about the same thing most reflects his heart. Youth ministry guru Mark Oestreicher (yes, he is a guru, and yes, he is the publisher of this book so you can do with that nugget of insight what you'd like) likes to talk about how, in his opinion and experience, most good youth ministries are weird. What he means is that just about every youth group is marked by one or two things that make them unique and different, and the really good youth groups are those that recognize their unique quirks and leverage them in a way that sets up their ministry to teenagers for success. I agree. I also think there are a few things that should be found in every youth group. Things that don't rely on theology, size of group, denomination, philosophy of ministry etc. I'm sure that list is actually fairly long, and I'm also quite confident that toward the very top of the list we'd find consistency, empathy, and grace. There's nothing weird about that!

THOUGHTS FROM A VOLUNTEER
by Paul Dempster

One constant in my ministry is a rubber chicken. I always keep one in my car and have one at every small group. Why a chicken? It's random, unexpected, and disruptive. There are so many creative uses for a rubber chicken—it becomes a talking stick where only the person holding the chicken can talk, it can be used in many different games, it can be an implement of discipline—in love of course. Most small groups I've led name the chicken. "Quaw" was one of my favorites.

On a more serious note, consistency is most often demonstrated not just through the constant of a rubber chicken, but simply by showing up, even when I'm tired, have had a crummy day, or feel less than well-prepared to lead a lesson. It means being on time, being prepared, and following a similar pattern each week. Cheering kids on in the activities they value outside of group, either in person or with an encouraging note or text.

Every young person is unique and it's important to gauge where they each are socially, spiritually, and emotionally. It is easier to empathize with people we feel connected to. I use open-ended questions to minimize the single word responses of "good," "fine," "yes," "no." Rather than asking, "How was your week" I'll ask, "What was the most interesting/funny/frustrating thing that happened to you this week?" It is important to create a safe place where teenagers can share ideas, concerns, hurts, and feelings; my role is less about teaching and more about leading open discussion, which communicates to them that their voices matter.

One year I had three boys out of ten who had lost their dads, something I'd never experienced. I couldn't fix this, and I couldn't be a surrogate dad for them, but I could listen. I could encourage them and I could positively model being a male who loves Jesus. It was that year when I started a tradition with my eighth graders that's continued on since: I teach them how to tie a necktie. It's a basic life skill, and those boys who had lost their dads reminded me that someone needed to teach it to them.

Another year I was assigned what I call a grab bag of kids. No two attended the same school, and aside from our small group they didn't see each other during the week. It was a challenge to bring the group together. They were a very physical group and a few had challenging social skills. To build empathy and comradery in our group, I introduced Romans 12:4: the body is made of many parts and we each have an essential role to play. Rather than read and talk about it, we experienced it. I walked our group to a nearby park and created two teams and assigned to each person a specific body part: eye, ear, mouth, feet, hands. They were instructed that they could only do what their assigned body part did—only the mouth could talk, only the ear could hear, and all but one guy was blindfolded to ensure that only the eye could see. Each team of body parts had to move about twenty feet as a group/blob and pick up a ball (actually a rubber chicken, of course) and bring it back. With no more instructions than that, each team had to work together. One team had everyone get on top of the two guys who were the legs, which was hilarious. That exercise taught an important Bible verse but also united our group through a memorable experience, and helped us learn more about each other. Our connections grew from there. It was the Holy Spirit who brought that group together in such a dramatic way.

Paul Dempster has been a volunteer in student ministries with junior highers for twenty-one years. When not hanging out with teenagers, his day job is leading the sales and marketing activities for a video camera manufacturer supporting the medical devices industry. He has two grown daughters and four grandkids, and both sons-in-law are youth pastors.

CHAPTER 8
TEACH LIKE IT ACTUALLY MATTERS

Right now you might be thinking, "I can skip this short (but probably super awesome) chapter on teaching because everybody knows teaching is overrated and teenagers don't remember the lessons, anyway." Don't think that; if you do, you're wrong.

Before I share a few tips about teaching, let me lead with this: In youth ministry, everything teaches something. Don't make the mistake of thinking the twenty to thirty minutes your youth group sets aside for the message or Bible study is the only time teaching and learning are taking place. Everything that happens in the context of your youth group is teaching your teenagers important lessons, lessons that concern virtually every aspect of life and faith. When newcomers are welcomed warmly, hospitality is taught. When the troublemaker is given a second chance, grace has been taught. When tough questions are welcomed, you are teaching teenagers that your youth group is a safe place to wonder and doubt. When you kiss your spouse in the youth room you are modeling a healthy marriage and the fact that old people still have a little gas in the tank.

While it's true that these types of lessons may be remembered as long as or longer than what's taught in your formal teaching time, it would be a massive mistake to underestimate the importance and power of a well-executed lesson. The moment will arrive, if it hasn't already, when you are expected to present some sort of lesson to teenagers. These tips will help you get ready for your big moment. For those of you who have been teaching teenagers for years, perhaps these will serve as important reminders:

3 BIGGIES IN A BOX
"WINGING IT" IS LAZY
LEAVE 'EM WANTING MORE
MIX IT UP

"Winging It" Is Lazy

I've heard every possible excuse (and used a few myself) for youth workers' lack of preparation heading into the lesson time:

"I don't prep because I like to let the Holy Spirit lead me." Lazy.

"I've discovered the best lessons are the ones I don't prepare...they feel more organic." Lazy.

"I let the group decide what they want to talk about, then we just figure it out as we go." Lazy.

"If I prep, I take it for granted...winging it keeps me on my toes." Lazy.

"Our group uses curriculum that does all the hard work for me!" Lazy.

"I'm too busy to prep." Lazy.

Every time I'm tempted to phone it in, freestyle, or "wing it," I remind myself of a few powerful Scriptures that emphasize the power of God's Word and the importance of approaching the teaching of it appropriately.

For the word of God is alive and powerful. It is sharper than the sharpest two-edged sword, cutting between soul and spirit, between joint and marrow. It exposes our innermost thoughts and desires. Hebrews 4:12

It is the same with my word. I send it out, and it always produces fruit. It will accomplish all I want it to, and it will prosper everywhere I send it. Isaiah 55:11

Dear brothers and sisters, not many of you should become teachers in the church, for we who teach will be judged more strictly. James 3:1

Work hard so you can present yourself to God and receive his approval. Be a good worker, one who does not need to be ashamed and who correctly explains the word of truth. 2 Timothy 2:15

Teenagers come to your youth group for all sorts of reasons: because their friends are there, because they love the music, because it's a safe respite from the rest of their world, because there are caring adults in the room. One or two may actually come to youth group because they look forward to a lesson or message from the Bible. But please don't make the mistake of deciding that since most teenagers don't come to youth group for the lessons, the lessons don't matter.

I was in high school when I first saw a bumper sticker I've seen hundreds of times since. I thought it was corny then, and I think it's corny now. But just because something's corny doesn't mean it isn't true. "DO YOUR BEST AND LET GOD DO THE REST."

Corny. But true. And when it comes to teaching, I'm not suggesting you need to be the best—I'm simply suggesting that God's Word, and the power it packs, deserves for us to do our best when preparing to teach it.

Teaching: Do your best! And let God do the rest.

Leave 'Em Wanting More
Leave them wanting more is one of my favorite leadership axioms. It's a reminder that too much of a good thing is rarely a good thing. When I was in college, I went to my buddy's house for

dinner. His mom was a fantastic cook; food was one of the love languages of their family. After dinner as we were unwinding and watching television, his mom walked in with a huge basket full of warm, homemade, cinnamon-flavored tortilla chips and encouraged me to "eat as many as you want!" So I did (I was taught to obey my elders). They were delicious, and over the next thirty minutes I must have eaten two pounds' worth of warm, homemade, cinnamon-flavored tortilla chips. About an hour later I got a stomachache and headed to the bathroom where I proceeded to throw up two pounds' worth of warm, homemade, cinnamon-flavored tortilla chips. To this day, I can't eat churros, or anything that reminds me of warm, homemade, cinnamon-flavored tortilla chips.

She should have left me wanting more. What if my friend's mom had said, "Kurt, these are delicious, but you can only have one serving"? Had she done so, I would have left my friend's house that evening hoping to return sometime soon for more warm, homemade, cinnamon-flavored tortilla chips. Instead, I've spent an entire lifetime avoiding anything that remotely resembles them! In fact, and this is no joke, just typing that story has made me a little bit nauseous.

Teaching God's Word to a group of teenagers is a good thing. A group of teenagers hearing an older, caring adult share a message or seeing them lead a Bible study is a good thing. But too much of a good thing is rarely a good thing.

Don't wing it. But don't swing the pendulum so far in the other direction that you prepare sixty-minute messages that no teenager could understand without a seminary degree and the ability to read the original Greek and Hebrew. Don't make the mistake of deciding that the only way to make the ninety-minute youth meeting worth everybody's time is to spend eighty-nine of those minutes doing a verse-by-verse exegetical study of the Book of Numbers.

Youth ministry guru Doug Fields likes to joke that there are only three topics teenagers want to learn about in church: Sex, end times, and whether there will be sex in the end times. He's right, unless you decide you are going to spend all of your time teaching those topics. Suddenly, something they were so interested in becomes something they may never want to think about again (warm, homemade, cinnamon-flavored tortilla chips).

Teach in such a way that you always leave them wanting more. Here are some helpful guidelines:

- Make sure the teaching time is learner-focused, not teacher-focused.
- Teach on topics they want to learn about and topics relevant to their daily lives.
- Keep your lessons short.
- Tell stories and include humor.
- Teach in series so you can spend two hours on an important topic over a four-week period, instead of trying to force it all into one long lesson.

Mix It Up
This goes along with leaving them wanting more, but is different enough to warrant some attention of its own.

In our early years of ministry and marriage, my wife, Rachel, and I served at a wonderful church. In fact, it was the same church she grew up in, the church I started attending in high school, and the church in which we met and were married. Our pastor was an amazing preacher with a gift for evangelism. Virtually every message he preached revolved around our need for God's gift of forgiveness through Jesus Christ. Every message ended with an opportunity for people to respond to the nudging of the Holy Spirit and surrender their lives to the ways of Jesus. (If Greg Stier is reading this I'm sure he's shouting, "Now we're talking, Kurt!") He did so because he believed it was his responsibility as a pastor to never present God's Word without giving folks an opportunity to yield their lives to Jesus. Fair enough. I have zero quarrel with that.

But there was an unintended consequence. Something as powerful and amazing as the gospel became predictable, almost boring. You see, my pastor had ONE way of presenting the gospel, ONE way of making his appeal, ONE way to respond. And he presented it all the exact same way over and over and over again. If it's possible to do so (I'm no theologian), my pastor had managed to inoculate his church to the most powerful of messages. If he had mixed it up a little bit, things might have been different. What if one Sunday while I was sleeping through his message he had said, "You know, on second thought, you really don't need Jesus after all!"? That would have grabbed my attention! Of course he would have pivoted to why, in fact, we do need Jesus—but by mixing it up just a little bit he would have grabbed our attention and piqued our interest.

The temptation of every teacher is to overuse the tools and methods with which they are most adept. When you do this, your greatest asset can begin to work against you because it becomes ordinary...expected. My pastor's greatest gift was his ability to present the gospel, but because he did it all the time, always in the same awesome way, it became ordinary and expected.

Mix it up! If you are super funny and your lessons are marked by humor, shock your audience by telling a few less jokes once in a while. If you love object lessons and utilize them better than anybody on the planet, mix it up by doing a simple lesson on one Bible verse. If your teenagers tell you that nobody has the depth and perspective that you have, turn the tables and ask for their perspectives during the lesson.

Do what works. Lean into your strengths. But mix it up from time to time in order to keep things fresh. Leave them wanting more, and leave them guessing what next week's lesson might be like!

If you want to be the best volunteer youth worker in the history of the world, you need to teach like it matters every time…because it does.

THOUGHTS FROM A VOLUNTEER
by Kim Tjepkema

Outside of building relationships with teenagers, the most important thing for me as a youth ministry volunteer is teaching them that the Bible offers excellent instruction on how to live their best lives.

My primary teaching role is to lead my small group of girls on Wednesday nights. When I approach the lesson for the week, the basis for which is provided by our youth ministry team, I first study the material for myself. I usually do this over the weekend. On Mondays I spend time mulling over the provided Scriptures and questions, thinking about my teens and how the lesson applies personally to each of them. On Tuesdays I try to map out my plan for our time together. This isn't something I like to do totally on my own—I always call or text my coleader, and at times other leaders, to gather any insight I missed or other ideas that might be helpful. I've learned that other leaders are gifted in bringing things to life, and it's always worth reaching out if I am stuck or could use input. Wednesday is review day. This is usually on the way to our small group, when I take fifteen minutes in my car to go over everything again. I've found that when I take the time to prep and reflect, there are always good outcomes for me as a leader and for the girls I lead.

Once our group is meeting, attention spans are short and chatter abounds! The lessons have to meet this energy level. Our lessons are chock-full of ice breakers, activities, Scriptures, and questions. If I did every single thing each lesson offered I would be doing a lot of the talking and I'd lose their attention, so it's important to edit. I have learned that I don't have to do it all in order to lead well. When tailoring a lesson to my group, I choose the best Scripture passages and questions that apply. I try to do twenty percent of the talking and leave the rest of it to them. I lead by asking a lot of questions.

One other win with my group is journaling. Giving these girls ten minutes to respond to the lesson through journaling allows them to make it personal. Leading teens to think through what the Bible teaches about life and how to live through good, applicable questions and a time of reflection with journaling leaves them wanting more. At the end of the year I give them these journals to keep, an experience that is a gift for me and for them.

I am always trying to mix it up to keep it interesting. One of my favorite things to do is raise up leaders within the group and bring in their voices to what we are learning. When I prep for a lesson I will bring a teenager onboard to help lead, sending them a question or two in advance to think over, along with Scripture that applies. The girls in our group enjoy hearing from their peers. And quite honestly, sometimes they're better at listening to their peers than to me!

There are also tons of resources online. I have used videos, podcasts, and tweets to help reinforce what we are learning. In my experience, teenagers are always interested in media. Using online materials keeps their attention and introduces them to a resource they can go to on their own. I also sometimes send my group home with homework. One of my favorite memories was when we asked our groups to find Scripture on friendship. The next week we gathered and the teenagers led. They each answered the question, "What does friendship look like?" based on the Scripture they found. We had the best discussion and the majority was student-led. Mixing it up keeps things interesting and meaningful for all of us.

TEACH LIKE IT ACTUALLY MATTERS

As a volunteer youth worker my goal is to model and teach what it looks like to pursue Jesus. I equip teenagers to seek out Scriptures and teachings on their own, ask good questions of themselves, apply Scripture to their current life situations, and reflect through journaling. Teaching matters!

Kim Tjepkema has been a volunteer youth worker for over seven years. When not spending time with teenagers, Kim is raising them. She's a mom to a twenty-one-year-old, nineteen-year-old, fifteen-year-old, and eleven-year-old, and has been happily married to Travis for twenty-six years.

HOW TO BE **THE BEST** VOLUNTEER YOUTH WORKER

CHAPTER 9
DON'T GET DEFLATED BY FLAT TIRES

The summer of 1988 was winding down. I was twenty-two years old and had just accepted a position as our church's first-ever junior high pastor. I decided my first official act in my new role would be to take two of my eighth grade guys, Chad and Joe, on an end-of-summer surf trip. We'd wake up early, spend a good chunk of the morning on the road, and catch some warm waves to wrap up a fun summer. We'd be sure to be home by 3:00 because Chad had a family outing he could not be late for. No worries; it would be an epic start to my new career.

It was. For all the wrong reasons. Here is a brief synopsis of everything that went awry on our way to the beach:

- I woke up early. Got to Chad's house. He wasn't awake. Had to wait.
- Chad and I got to Joe's house. He wasn't awake. Had to wait.
- Got a flat tire about twenty minutes into the trip.
- Spent thirty minutes searching my car for a jack. No jack.
- Spent another thirty minutes trying to flag down help.
- After changing the tire, drove about ten miles before the spare suffered a blowout.
- We jumped the freeway fence, then walked a mile through a

- horrific part of town looking for tire store while "rolling" a flat tire alongside us.
- Rolled the new tire back through town for a mile and installed it on the car.
- Back on the freeway, I double-checked with the boys to ensure they had each packed a lunch. They had each failed to pack a lunch.
- Stopped by grocery store to purchase lunch supplies.
- Purchasing lunch supplies took about three times as long as it should have because, well, eighth-grade boys.
- Halfway to the beach Chad pointed out that my gas gauge was below empty.
- I confidently told Chad that my gas gauge was broken and we were fine.
- We weren't fine.

By the time we finally got to the beach I realized that in order to get Chad home by 3:00, we didn't have time to surf. Leaving the boards strapped to the roof, the three of us sprinted to the water, bodysurfed for about fifteen minutes, and loaded ourselves back into the car to start the two-hour drive back home. Ugh.

I started the day as a hope-filled, confident young youth worker and dropped into bed that night questioning every aspect of my calling. How could I be an effective junior high pastor when I couldn't even pull of an event for two kids? I hadn't thought through the timing, the details, or any alternate plans for if something went wrong. Even worse, I had let Chad and Joe down. The promise of a fun day of surfing had turned into a day marked by one fiasco after another. I felt like quitting before I had really even started.

Fast forward ten years. It's 1998 and I'm somehow a decade into a youth ministry career. Rachel and I are in our first year of ministry at Saddleback Church when we get an invitation to a wedding of a former teenager from our first ministry setting, Chad and Joe's church. I was certain they'd both be at the wedding and looked forward to seeing them again after so many years. Sure enough, during the reception the three of us found ourselves reminiscing about their junior high years and Chad naturally brought up our surf trip. After reliving every. single. painful. moment, Chad said something I will never forget: "Guys, our junior high group was the best!"

Wait, what? The best? Sure, if it's opposite day and "best" somehow means "very worst" at doing things like taking junior highers to the beach.

I tell that story quite often because it's full of lessons for youth workers. Lesson one: Always have a tire jack in your car. But out of all the lessons this story teaches, one seems to stand out: Don't get deflated by flat tires.

You will have rough moments. Things will go wrong. Events will flop. Lessons will land flat. Parents will complain. The sound system will get hit by dodgeballs. Elders won't understand why youth ministry matters. The music will be too loud. Or too quiet. Or there won't be music at all because the sound system got hit by dodgeballs.

How do you keep yourself from being completely deflated by the flat tires of youth ministry? Here are a few tips:

3 BIGGIES IN A BOX

BOUNCE BACK!
FALL FORWARD
THE WORST MOMENTS OFTEN CREATE THE BEST MEMORIES

Bounce Back!
I once attended a workshop on the topic of longevity in ministry. It focused on why some manage to stick it out and others don't.

We looked at case studies, compared various ministry categories, and investigated stories of people in volunteer, part-time, and full-time roles.

And while there is obviously a myriad of contributing factors to one's ability to stay in ministry for the long haul, if I had to boil it all down to one concept—one word, even—it would simply be resilience. A dictionary definition of resilience is "an ability to recover from or adjust easily to misfortune or change."[2] I'd define it even more simply: "the ability to bounce back."

Youth ministry is full of pitfalls and potholes. It's rife with opportunities to get it wrong, disappoint people, and come up short. I lead a junior high small group every Wednesday night and virtually every week I find a few ways to get it wrong, disappoint people, and come up short! Nothing makes me question my calling and effectiveness as a youth worker more than that ninety-minute time slot of my week. But I've learned how to be resilient and to recover quickly from difficulties. I've learned the art of bouncing back after setbacks.

As I plopped into bed back after a horrific first attempt at being a junior high pastor in 1988, all sorts of thoughts raced through my mind. At the top of the list was whether I was cut out for youth ministry after all. Was I really called? Did the church know what it was doing when it hired me? Did I have what it took? Frankly, in that moment I didn't know the answers but I knew this: I wasn't about to give up. I refused to let a flat tire keep me deflated.

Your time will come. You'll mess up. Something will go wrong. You will question your fruitfulness. Your tire will go flat. Bounce back.

Fall Forward
A few chapters ago I shared that I was assigned the role of running back on my freshmen football team, even though I had zero running back experience. Because I had zero experience, my

learning curve was huge and I was determined to learn as much as possible so I could be the very best below-average freshman running back our school had ever seen.

The same day I was given that role, I pulled our coach aside and asked him to give me the single most important tip to being a good running back. I was certain the answer would have something to do with being big, fast, and strong. I was equally certain I wouldn't qualify. His answer was shockingly simple. "Johnston, the key to being a great running back is to always fall forward. Whenever you get hit, do your very best to fall forward and gain some positive yardage. Now, go get me a cigarette." Okay, he didn't say the part about the cigarette, but it was the early '80s so he could have.

"Fall forward." That's good advice for a high school running back, and it's good advice for youth workers, too! "…gain some positive yardage." Yep! But how? How can you ensure that you fall forward and gain positive yardage as a leader and youth worker when things go wrong? How can you be sure to bounce back in the right direction? Here are three questions I ask myself every time I suffer a ministry flat tire:

- **What Went Wrong?**
  Identify the source of the "flat tire." Was it poor planning? Were expectations unclear? Were guidelines and directives not followed? Was it simply a bad idea? Did I misread the audience? Was it something I never saw coming that was out of my control? Was it something I SHOULD have seen coming? When answering this question, I try not to assign blame, but I do want to identify the source of the flat tire.

- **What Can I Learn?**
  Leaders are learners. And one of the best ways to avoid making the same mistake over and over again is to learn from the mistake you just made. When something goes wrong, many leaders quickly dust themselves off and move

on without taking the time to evaluate and reflect (I have this tendency). But if we don't identify the source of the problem and ask what lessons we can learn, we are destined to make the same mistake again and again.

I've had the joy of coleading junior high small groups with Tom Wheeler for years. "Coleading" may be a stretch; the reality is that Tom leads and I show up once in a while. Tom is my age, a successful engineer who has designed the majority of our city's public spaces. He is highly involved in all sorts of ministry projects with his wife. Both of us drag ourselves into small group every week drained from our various responsibilities. We both really like leading a junior high small group, but we are old and tired.

Heading into the new season of small groups, we realized that something was not clicking. We identified the majority of the problem: We had a super energetic group of guys who were being led by two old guys. Our solution? Enlist the world's coolest twelfth grader to help us out. Enter Carter Coppes. Carter has in spades everything Tom and I lack. Energy, relevance…hair. And while Carter hasn't solved all of our group's problems (slacker), he has made a significant difference in the overall experience the group gives our guys. Because Tom and I were willing to ask what was going wrong and learn a few things, our group is finally beginning to gain positive yardage.

- **What Changes Can I Make So It Doesn't Happen Again?**
  Don't get me wrong; I think older youth workers often make the best youth workers. Saddleback's original member from back in 1980, Don Dale, currently serves as one of our volunteers and is amazing. But Tom and I realized that in our setting, having a young leader worked really well, and we have changed our mindset to ensure we never find ourselves leading a junior high small group without somebody a little younger to offset our age and mellowness.

Our small group was suffering a flat tire.

> What went wrong? Our guys weren't connecting with the experience.
>
> What can we learn? Tom and I were getting older.
>
> What changes can we make? Let's get Carter to help...he's super cool!

The Worst Moments Often Create The Best Memories
On the way home from the wedding reception I shared with Rachel what Chad had said. "Guys, our junior high group was the best!"

Because this scenario had happened before we were married and because I had tried for a while to block it out of my mind, she had never heard the story. I recounted every painful detail to get her up to speed. Cheap therapy, I suppose.

For Chad, our junior high group wasn't the best because we had a gym, or because our lessons were great, or because I told somewhat funny jokes on a regular basis. Somehow, in some weird way, the memory of a horrifically executed day of surfing translated into a junior high ministry that in Chad's mind was *"the best."* While I don't know for sure how that played out in his mind, here's what I do know: Moments create memories. Awesome youth ministry moments create powerful memories, which is why things like summer camp, mission trips, and experiential learning opportunities are so important. After all, everything teaches something and lessons are caught, not taught. We've all seen this truth played out over and over again.

But it's important to remember that even the worst moments can create good memories. In fact, depending on how we respond to them, the worst moments often create the best memories. One of my worst moments in youth ministry created one of Chad's very best youth ministry memories. That's weird math. Weird math that all adds up perfectly when we remember how deeply most teenagers value relationships and experiences.

Effective youth ministry is built on memories.

And maybe the best youth ministry is built on the memories that begin with a flat tire.

THOUGHTS FROM A VOLUNTEER
by Carter Coppes

I grew up going to church every weekend with my parents, but it was during junior high when I became more involved. Ever since then, I have wanted to serve with junior highers. I viewed my leaders as the coolest people on earth and hoped to be just like them.

I started serving with my church's junior high ministry last year when I was a junior in high school, partnering as a coleader with adults. I was super excited to jump right in and have a blast. At first, however, it was more difficult than I had imagined. I did not know any of the kids, and they seemed uncomfortable around me when I tried to talk with them or sit with them. My first couple of months were discouraging because I saw other leaders connecting way better with junior highers than I was.

I wanted to build relationships with junior highers like I'd had with my old leaders, but I now realize that I was not willing to be patient. I wanted the connections to happen right away. Plus, I was not putting in as much time and effort as other leaders before and after our official gatherings to get to know the kids.
Even though I felt discouraged, I committed to lead a cabin at summer camp. I prayed that I would develop strong connections with the boys in my cabin group. After a slow first day getting up

to the camp and meeting all of them, it turned out to be a blast. Even though it got kind of annoying to sleep in a cabin with twelve junior high boys (not the most ideal scenario for rest!), it was the time and commitment I needed to start developing relationships with my group. From worship to talking in cabin time to destroying them in paintball, camp allowed me to get to know these boys in fun and serious ways.

The boys in the cabin started seeking me out, asking me questions about whatever was on their minds and wanting me to go with them to try new games and activities. After camp, I felt that my tires were full of air, no longer as deflated as they were when I started as a leader. I grew to understand that it takes time and patience to build relationships. Junior highers, like most people, are at first uncomfortable talking to new faces. That isn't a problem, it's just part of the process.

Fast forward about a month to my senior year when I took another step and became the life group leader for the guys who had been in my cabin. I think it's remarkable that I went from being a disappointing leader the year before (or at least it felt that way to me) to leading a small group just six months later. Now we're spending time together playing tag at the park, getting frozen yogurt, and playing mafia, and I'm teaching them about the Bible. Our relationships have grown with time together and it's almost like the frustrating and awkward interactions never happened. Thankfully, I was able to learn from those difficult early experiences and grow as a leader through them instead of giving up. Leading this group of guys is one of the best decisions I've ever made. Even though it can be difficult to quiet down junior high boys, it is totally worth it. I've learned that it takes time, patience, and consistency to be the best leader you can be.

Carter Coppes has been a volunteer with junior highers for a little over a year. When not volunteering at the church he is doing schoolwork or at the beach surfing.

CHAPTER 10
STICK AROUND

When I was in my early thirties I spoke at a large youth ministry training event teaching a workshop on junior high ministry. As was my habit, I left about fifteen minutes at the end of my presentation for question and answer time. I loved doing this because A) it allowed participants to get additional insights into something I'd presented or ask a question about an area of ministry I hadn't covered and B) because it meant I could prepare fifteen minutes less content. I'll let you decide which of those two was the higher motivation for me.

Because I'd presented similar material at numerous events over the years, I already knew the questions that would be asked, questions about finding more volunteers, handling disruptive teens, gaining support from the senior leadership, etc. Very few questions about junior high ministry could be asked that I didn't have a little bit of experience with and feel confident answering.

All was going well. Typical questions. Typical answers. Until the very last one. A young man in his early twenties eagerly raised his hand. I like eager hand-raisers, so I called on him. (That, plus the fact that his was the only hand in the air.)

"Kurt, I want to be a lifelong junior high worker like you. How do I do that?"

Lifelong like me? I was barely thirty years old! What did I know about "lifelong" anything, yet alone lifelong junior high ministry? Because I was caught off guard by a question I had never heard before, one I had never even considered, I gave the most honest answer I could.

"I'm not sure. I'll let you know if I ever become a lifelong junior high worker myself."

He wasn't impressed. I know that because he made one of those snarky, squishy faces people make when they aren't impressed.

Now that I'm in my fifties, the question of longevity in youth ministry—how I've managed to stick around all these years—is the most popular question I get asked. I understand it. In the world of youth ministry I'm a unicorn of sorts. A short, bald unicorn. It's a question worth asking because we all want to experience fulfillment and fruitfulness through our involvement in youth ministry, and a fair amount of that comes from sticking around for a while.

The title of this little book is *How to Be the Best Volunteer Youth Worker in the History of the World*, but obviously there's no way to quantify that. Plus, I can't afford the cost of the size of trophy that person would deserve if we could actually identify him or her. But I know this: If we were to give out that award, it wouldn't go to somebody who served for six months. It would go to somebody who stuck around, who served for the long haul, who determined it was worth the effort.

I still don't know for certain what it takes to be a lifelong youth worker. I haven't accomplished that yet. But I have learned a few things along my journey toward that destination that might help you stick around for a while, too:

STICK AROUND

3 BIGGIES IN A BOX

PUT THIS BOOK INTO PRACTICE
HAVE A LONG VIEW
IGNORE THE OFF-RAMPS

Put This Book Into Practice

If this is the only youth ministry book you've ever read, it's the best youth ministry book you've ever read. You're welcome. If you've read other books on this topic you know the truth. Either way, you've made it this far and invested a little bit of your time in being a learner. I'm flattered that you would read something I wrote, but more importantly I hope some of what you've read has struck a chord in you. I hope you want to put some of what you've read into practice in your ministry setting. I love the wisdom found in Ecclesiastes 10:10 (NIV):

If the ax is dull and its edge unsharpened, more strength is needed, but skill will bring success.

Pretend you are standing in front of a big pile of logs that need to be split into firewood. Not sure how best to go about your task, you look around and see an old ax sitting nearby. Upon further inspection, you notice that the ax is incredibly dull. Good news... you know how to sharpen an ax! This scenario presents you with a few options:

- Decide you don't want firewood after all.
- Decide you don't want to sharpen the ax, and proceed using the dull ax.
- Take the time to sharpen the ax before getting down to choppin' business.

I'm from Southern California, so I really have no idea if this analogy makes sense. I buy my firewood at a grocery store. But I believe the Bible, and I'm pretty confident the above passage isn't really meant to give us wood-chopping advice, but rather provide us with some godly wisdom about the benefits of being lifelong learners, sharpening our "axes," and putting those skills into practice.

By the way, the passage immediately following Ecclesiastes 10:10 is a reminder that if a snake bites before it is charmed, the charmer shouldn't get paid. Words to live by, especially if you happen to be a snake charmer.

My earnest prayer as I've been writing is that God would use this little book to sharpen your youth ministry ax, and that you would start swinging away! Youth ministry is hard work, and people often get tired, frustrated, and worn out long before they need to simply because their ax is dull.

Have A Long View
Beyond reminding us that the worst moments often create the best memories, my surf trip disaster story may teach a bigger lesson to youth workers. It's a perfect example of our need to have a long view. You and I are in the seed-planting business. Our job is to view every opportunity we have with teenagers—whether it's teaching a lesson, leading a mission trip, or struggling through a disastrous surf outing—as an opportunity to plant little seeds of things like faith, hope, perspective, and truth into the hearts of our students. And while doing so, we need to remind ourselves that the seeds we plant often take years to take root, to grow, and to produce fruit.

I've noticed that when I feel like giving up, or am convinced I'm too old to work with teenagers, more often than not I'm focusing on short-term, immediate frustrations. I'm wondering why I'm not immediately getting the results I think I'm supposed to be getting.

I'm writing this book in a coffee shop near our church. Ten minutes ago I ordered a drink and the barista, whom I didn't recognize, called me by name. She introduced herself and shared that she is graduating from seminary in a few months. Very cool. Then she said, "I was in Saddleback's junior high ministry back in the day, and I just want you to know how formative that experience was for me."

She went on to rave about her junior high small group leader, Natalie Hall, who poured into her, believed in her, and constantly reminded her that she was a handcrafted masterpiece for whom God had big things planned. Natalie was planting seeds! Natalie now lives in the Philippines where her husband, Matt, serves as the campus pastor for one of our international campuses. My hunch is she has no idea that the seeds she planted so long ago are bearing fruit in the life of a young barista back home.

And I'm not going to tell her because I'm gonna tease her with the beginning of the story and tell her she needs to buy this book in order to hear the ending!

Ignore The Off-Ramps

When asked what it takes to stick around as a youth worker, I used to feel the pressure (mostly self-imposed, I'm sure) to have an impressive response that included a healthy balance of theology, calling, passion, and commitment. The truth is, the response I had crafted was more for me than it was for the person asking the question. I was trying to convince myself that what I've committed my entire adult life to is worth it. I mean, is youth ministry really a calling? Is it really something that makes a kingdom impact? Is it worth saying no to other ministry opportunities in order to stay involved in the lives of teenagers? Is embracing the squiggle something worth giving my life to? I needed the answer to be a resounding YES, so I made sure my answer to the question packed a punch.

I have a different answer now. I've realized that lasting in youth ministry is easier than it sounds. If you want to last, you can! As long as you aren't stealing money from the offering or strapping teenagers to the roof of your car, you are largely in control of the longevity of your youth ministry season. (Speaking of strapping teenagers to the roof of your car…I did. It was my very first year of ministry and I thought it would be funny to strap a junior higher to my surf racks and drive through town. The junior higher's dad heard about it and actually laughed. Apparently, parents didn't love their children as much in the 1980s as they do today. My church didn't fire me. They should have.)

Today when I'm asked how to last in youth ministry, my answer is simple: Ignore the off-ramps.

As you drive down the freeway of youth ministry you will be presented with a variety of off-ramps, and it will make perfect sense to take any one of them:

- You get a promotion at work and it demands more of your time. Off-ramp.
- You take on a heavier study load in college. Off-ramp.
- You get married and decide you need to focus on your new marriage. Off-ramp.
- You have kids and decide you need to dedicate more quality time to them. Off-ramp.
- You turn forty and begin to feel a little old and tired. Off-ramp.
- You turn fifty and actually are a little old and tired. Off-ramp.
- Another ministry in the church asks you to help. Off-ramp.
- The paid youth pastor resigns and there is transition in the air. Off-ramp.
- Off-ramp. Off-ramp. Off-ramp. Off-ramp.

Obviously at some point all of us will see an off-ramp and sense that it's the one we truly need to take. But until then, if you want to stick around in youth ministry…just ignore the rest of the off-ramps!

Thanks for being a youth ministry volunteer. It matters, and you are making an eternal difference. Someday, I believe God will usher you into heaven with the words, "Well done, my good and faithful servant." And maybe, just maybe, he'll whisper in your ear, "By the way, you were the best volunteer youth worker in the history of the world."

Well, I promised my editor that this little book would be exactly 20,000 words so you will know I hit that mark when

THOUGHTS FROM A VOLUNTEER
by Rebecca MacLean

Having been the beneficiary of amazing youth volunteers pouring into our four children's lives and witnessing the impact that a mentor other than Mom and Dad can have on a kid, I decided to jump into youth ministry seven years ago. I am so glad I did! Since then, I have led three different groups of high school girls. Without sugarcoating the times when I have felt inadequate, too old, or simply worn out by feelings of great sadness for what these girls are experiencing in their personal lives, I can unequivocally say that being a youth worker has been one of my biggest joys. While I can probably get a thousand "amens" to the fact that leading teenagers can be tough, the reward and privilege of getting to walk hand in hand with these girls during their journey to knowing and loving Jesus far outweighs the difficult seasons of leadership.

Jesus's teaching of the law of the harvest has been an encouragement in times of discouragement. When I started leading seven years ago, I eagerly desired to see fruit from our weekly small group meetings. I wanted the girls to leave each night with a huge "Aha," or at the very least a nugget to ponder from our discussions. I wanted to have the girls fall in love with Jesus and for that to have an immediate impact on their life choices. In reality, this was more the exception than the rule. But a wise friend reminded me that we reap and sow in different seasons. This idea was a game changer for me and served to shift my perspective. My job was to simply love these girls and plant seeds of God's words in their hearts. It was God's job to do the rest.

The HARVEST: Today, I enjoy the benefits of great friendships with many of "my girls." I love grabbing coffee with them when they're home from college, and hearing about their lives after high school. Many of them are walking with Jesus and have owned their faith while they've been away from home. They come to me for advice, ask for podcast or book recommendations, and still ask some hard Jesus questions. There are others who are questioning their faith and are not currently pursuing a relationship with Jesus. But I trust that God is still working in their hearts and minds and that seeds planted in our weekly meetings during high school will bring a harvest at the right time. My love for the girls under my care is what propels me to stay connected, and to keep going even through the challenges. Even when there have been hard seasons in my own life (what Kurt might describe as off-ramps), or hard seasons within small group, I have found that being a mentor to these girls is always worth it. While I will always be their small group leader, I am overjoyed that they now call me friend.

Rebecca MacLean has been a high school youth volunteer for seven years. She's been married to her husband, Gordon, for twenty-six years and loves being a mom to their brood of four kids who are now ages sixteen through twenty-three.

Endnotes
1. Patrick Lencioni, *The Five Dysfunctions of a Team: A Leadership Fable* (Hoboken, NJ: Jossey-Bass, 2002).
2. "Resilience." Merriam-Webster.com. 2020. https://www.merriam-webster.com/dictionary/Resilience (May 2020).

Made in the USA
Middletown, DE
03 September 2023

37872792R00057